Citizens of the Cosmos

Citizens of the Cosmos

Life's Unfolding from Conception
through Death to Rebirth

BEREDENE JOCELYN

STEINERBOOKS
2009

2009
Published by SteinerBooks
610 Main Street, Great Barrington, MA 01230
www.steinerbooks.org

First published by
The Continuum Publishing Company, NY, 1981.

Library of Congress Cataloging-in-Publication Data is available.

ISBN 978-0-88010-633-7

Printed in the United States

CONTENTS

PREFACE

Imagine a person walking through a forest and coming upon thousands of stones set methodically into symmetrical patterns. Perhaps some of the formations indicate mathematical equations. The rational conclusion would be that an intelligent being had arranged the stones because such precise patterns do not form themselves randomly in nature.

Beredene Jocelyn perceived such patterns in everyday human life. Using astrology, she could see the rhythms and patterns orchestrated by the planets as they shaped a human life.

Beredene believed that this cosmic architecture was created by self-sacrificing divine beings and that humanity once existed in a primal spiritual form among these higher beings. At that time, humans were like infants, with no sense of "I." Also, there was no freedom. Gradually, humanity descended into matter, leaving behind the comfort and the awareness of the spiritual world. The parabolic blueprint of human evolution, calls for our rising to a fully conscious spiritual existence after we have struggled through and transformed evil and materialism. The ascent begins with our becoming spiritually intelligent.

Citizens of the Cosmos was written with the intention of helping us to become spiritually conscious and intelligent.

In her October 1982 newsletter, Beredene responded to the question, "What can I do in these troubled times?"

My first response was, "Become spiritually intelligent." That, of course, can be a lifetime process, but one can begin with basic knowledge about man as a being of body, soul, and spirit, and to know that he is related to the soul and spirit of the universe. Thus, we can livingly know and feel ourselves to be citizens of the cosmos. This expands our horizons far beyond what any university or cultural program can offer, and it enriches earthly life by intensely deepening our inner impulses...."

Citizens of the Cosmos not only reveals the Grand Design of life but brings us comfort in showing that higher beings are involved in our spiritual evolution. For this is the work of the higher beings: to create the rhythmic flows that affect our lives, showing us we are not alone.

Though Beredene laid down the astrological blueprint for an individual life, it is important to note that she would always say this only gives us indications, and that these are subject to a person's free will—a free will that yearns for its spiritual reunion with our creators.

Beredene's life was devoted to spiritual enrichment and to promoting good among all people. This wonderful book is a clearly written guide for life, as well as for the life beyond death. It is with great pleasure that *Citizens of the Cosmos* is presented to the public once again.

Rick Jacobs
February 20009

FOREWORD

When human beings and the universe are considered from the viewpoint of materialism only, the missing factors make it impossible to comprehend either the individuals or the cosmos in their wholeness.

It is heartening to know that attempts are being made to enlarge our understanding. A new and better picture of the human being is gained whenever missing elements are found. For years there has been a growing interest in thanatology, the science of dying and death. Valuable contributions have been made in this little-known area. The other pole of earth-life—birth and life before birth—is also beginning to receive attention.

Inquiry in recent years into what lies between birth and death has revealed that there are adult life cycles as well as stages of development in childhood. A leading psychologist, however, stated that a detailed portrayal of adult development is "years away, if one ever emerges at all from the stacks of case histories and statistics being accumulated."

Citizens of the Cosmos bears the good news that the detailed portrayal is not years away; it is here and now. For, this book presents you with the *key* to life's year-by-year unfolding from conception to death, the key also to the planetary spheres through which we pass from death to rebirth. It is hoped that once you possess the key, you will pursue further the vast cosmic-earthly-human treasures yet to be revealed.

Introduction

1

CITIZENS OF THE COSMOS—
UNKNOWINGLY OR KNOWINGLY

ONE day an elderly friend was talking and not noticing how she was buttoning her coat. She had started incorrectly. As she continued, all the buttons were being fastened in the wrong holes. When I called her attention to it, she laughingly and good-naturedly unbuttoned them and started all over again.

How wonderful it would be if we as readily and as good naturedly changed our deep-rooted views, once we found out that we began with the wrong premise! When we start with an incorrect premise in our conception of life and of the nature of human beings, then all our conclusions will necessarily follow one after another, forming a picture which is as out of balance as was my friend's coat. Let us illustrate this with three specific premises. (Here and throughout the book, the word "man" is used in its generic sense, indicating mankind as a whole.)

Premise 1: Man is Body Only

The premise with which many people begin, especially in the Western world, is that man is body only, without soul and without spirit, and that life begins with birth and ends with death. They think that there is nothing before birth, absolutely nothing, hence they have no qualm about abortion. As for after death, that too is zero, or at best a question mark.

Limited view of life

If one identifies oneself with the body, what conclusions naturally follow? One concept readily accepted is that man is a higher animal. Another is that heredity is all-important. Therefore to know who one is, one has to trace one's roots. No attention is given to one's own essential being as an individual apart from heredity.

From this premise there follows the attempt to educate children from infancy and to crowd as much as possible into the early years, disregarding the need for stages of gradual unfolding. This is like expecting fruit from a seedling!

On the basis that man is body only without soul, another conclusion, when carried to the extreme, is that there are no moral laws. Physical laws holding sway in the body and in the visible physical world are, of course, recognized. Spiritual laws and soul laws—that is, supersensible laws—that have to do with morality and with causal influences originating in physically invisible realms, are for a materialist no part of his reality. As a consequence, events are thought to be ruled by chance. What matters is that one "gets by," or "anything is all right as long as one does not get caught." Lacking moral responsibility and world-purpose, one tries to get all the earthly goods one can. All too often one judges people by what they have, rather than by what they are.

The soul-spiritual darkness, in which the materialistically minded live, engenders insecurity, discontent, distortion of values, emptiness, boredom, and fear. Hence "therapy" has become fashionable in our scientific age, substituting psychology for religion. Psychology literally means the science of the soul. Yet, paradoxically, shallow forms of psychology deny the existence of the soul! Behavioral patterns tend to be linked to physical factors—bodily, hereditary, or environmental—not to activities of the soul per se and the individualized spirit connected with worlds of soul and spirit. Since these worlds are denied, and since the only reality is this single earthlife, one of the greatest fears is the fear of death. If "I am my body and my body is I," it is logical to think, "I cease to exist when my body dies."

Premise 2: Man is Body and Soul

Premise 2, that the human being consists of body and soul, is the conventional Western religious view. After the Eighth Ecumenical Council of the Church (Constantinople IV) in 869 A.D., it became heretical to speak of man as threefold, consisting of body, soul, and spirit. Man was to be regarded as body and soul alone.

When seen in historical perspective, this was justified at a certain stage in the education of the human race. Partial views are necessary at certain stages of development in order to focus on specific faculties and to accomplish definite tasks. Even premise 1, that man is body only, is likewise justified for a limited time. The materialistic outlook in our age of natural science enabled the people of the West to master the physical world. And by shutting themselves off from the supersensible worlds and the guiding spiritual Beings, they became more *self*-conscious and independent (also more egotistic).

Inasmuch as the body is included in all premises, hereditary laws are valid, although with varying importance, in all conclusions. If one's view of the human being is that he or she has a soul as well as a body, then in addition to the natural laws governing the physical body and the physical world, there is recognition of the moral laws which apply to the soul and to the soul world. Hence there is a greater sense of responsibility, a more active conscience, and more purpose and meaning to life.

If there is faith in supersensible realities, souls have an inner light that dispels some of the doubts and fears that beset those who identify wholly with the physical realm. This light gives a sense of security, confidence, compassion, equanimity, and radiance.

However, as religion has increasingly adapted itself to science, and as materialism has so thoroughly penetrated modern thinking, a growing number of people who profess to believe that they have a soul, actually live as do those who identify themselves with the body alone. They have no surety about life after death. If they assert that the soul lives on after death, what lies beyond remains unknown. They are not prepared to face the death of loved ones with understanding and emotional stability.

Premise 3: Man is Body, Soul, and Spirit

Let us now start with a different premise and present another way of looking at life, one derived from spiritual-scientific investigation. The premise is that man is threefold, consisting of body, soul, and spirit.

Again, as in premises 1 and 2, heredity applies to the body, which is subject to the physical laws of birth and death. The spirit is birthless and deathless. The spirit is immortal, eternal, and governed by the law of reincarnation, that is, repeated earthlives. During earthlife the soul mediates between the body and the spirit. It is subject to the laws of self-created destiny. According to these laws we reap what we have sown, and in the present we are sowing what we shall reap in the future.

With the body we live in the physical world. With the soul we live in the supersensible, truly moral world and are accountable for

every seemingly secret thought, word, feeling, and deed. For a time
we may "get by" with a wrong action, but in the longer span of
repeated lives we have to face the consequences. When difficult
destiny occurs, the unenlightened persons of premises 1 and 2 ask,
"Why did this happen to me?" When we begin with premise 3, we
can accept our self-created destiny with equanimity and even gratitude.

An expanded view of humanity is inseparable from an expanded
view of the universe. Along with the exclusion of the spirit and soul
in the self, we have lost the spirit and soul of the world, and even
reduced the heavens to a vast mechanism to be explored by com-
plex machines alone. No matter how perfect the mechanized ex-
plorers are, they will never reveal more than the physical results of
the activities of supersensible Beings, not the spiritual Beings
themselves.

Without acknowledging the spirituality of the cosmos and the
ongoing individualized spirit in the human being, we cannot
rightly understand the truth of reincarnation. Increasingly the idea
of repeated earthlives is accepted with the attention focused almost
exclusively on the lives on earth, without any clarity about, or concern for, what happens in supersensible realms between the earthlives. Without the whole view, even acceptance of the truth of
reincarnation may be quite materialistic and also egotistic. Omitted
from the picture are the innumerable experiences we have in the
soul and spiritual worlds between each death and new birth, as
described in the second part of this book, "Our Journey Through the
Cosmos Between Death and Rebirth."

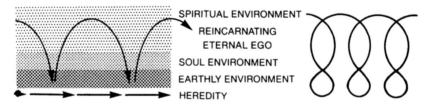

SPIRITUAL ENVIRONMENT

REINCARNATING
ETERNAL EGO

SOUL ENVIRONMENT

EARTHLY ENVIRONMENT

HEREDITY

Larger view of life connected with the cosmic environment

Between death and a new birth we are in a purely cosmic environment. In earthlife, too, we are still connected with this cosmic
environment in addition to the earthly one in which we live. This
enlarged view is illustrated in the following two diagrams, although
the spiraling form of the lemniscate (resembling the figure 8) must

be conceived as progressing in more than the two-dimensional plane of the drawing.

If this is the premise with which we start, the whole subject of life's unfolding will be approached very differently. If a person's essential being existed before birth and is eternal, then the parents provide only the physical germ, with its formative forces, and the material substances for the physical body. They neither create nor possess one's essential being. When I told this to a young man, he shook my hand gratefully. He had been made to believe that he was bound to his parents for everything. To know that there was something in him that was his very own, that was free from the heredity which had dwarfed his own potential, was comforting and encouraging to him. Yet we should remember that before conception, when we are preparing for our next earthlife, we choose the parents who will best suit our destiny needs.

This third premise enables us to walk on the earth not as the highest animal but as a citizen of the cosmos. The large numbers of mankind that hold to the first premise are unknowingly victims of a form of amnesia. They have no satisfactory answers to such questions as: Who am I? Where did I come from? Why am I here? They wander over the earth not knowing their true being, their real identity.

A dentist to whom I was sent for some specialized work voiced the view that death ends everything and that we completely drop out of existence. As soon as I was able to reply, I tried to explain that each individual is a vital part of the cosmos, which would be incomplete without every single soul. We are integrated into the universe as a part of an evolving whole, and we cannot escape from it any more than can the earth escape from the cosmos. Whether we know it or not, we are citizens of the cosmos.

It is important to realize that there are no clear lines of demarcation between the conclusions as practiced in the lives of some of the people who hold the three premises presented here. Most of the older generation grew up with premise 2. Younger people may have started with 2 and changed to 1 on entering college. As materialism penetrated more deeply into all avenues of our culture, not only did children grow up knowing only premise 1, but materialistic thinking so thoroughly permeated the lives of everyone that it will take a long time to bring about a complete change to a spiritual conception. It is somewhat like defrosting a refrigerator; just when we think it is all defrosted, we find at the back a piece of unmelted ice.

Today, while writing this, I received a letter from a sincere student of the science of the spirit. She described her recent visit with an old friend who for years was the Episcopal bishop of one of our largest cities, and who now is terminally ill in a nursing home in her area. "His questions about dying were addressed to me rather than the priest who comes with communion daily." Gratefully she recalled "the delight the old man has when I have talked to him about the spiritual world and his smiling satisfaction when my answers literally 'warmed his soul'!"

A promising sign for the future is that a "new breed" of young people is being born. They have, as it were, premise 3 already "built in" and come as spiritual knowers. As premises 1 and 2 were justified in the light of historical development, so now in our twentieth century it is needful, if earth evolution is to progress, that premise 3 replace premises 1 and 2. Only a spiritual conception of the cosmos and of the individual as a threefold being can awaken in our materially oriented and scientifically trained civilization the realization that there are moral and spiritual laws in addition to natural laws to which humanity must hearken. A knowledge of these laws could restore order to our growing social chaos.

With different emphases, the third premise was the accepted world-view in ancient times, as it still is, to a large extent, in the East today. Foremost of all was the spirit, and least of all the body— the spirit was real and the body an illusion. The relationship to the cosmos was instinctive and more real than that to the earth. Not until the Incarnation of the Christ, the Cosmic I AM, in the Greco-Roman civilization, did individuals become mature for the indwelling, self-conscious I. And only in Roman times did they for the first time regard themselves as citizens of an earthly state. We now live in the era when we can be fully ego-conscious *citizens of the cosmos*.

> The light of cosmic being
> On thine own I
> Bestow,
> For free and active willing,
> And thou wilt truly *think*
> In human-spirit being.
> —RUDOLF STEINER

2

CHANGING CONSCIOUSNESS AND CHANGING WORLD-PICTURES

IF YOU ever returned to the scene of your childhood you may have been amazed at how different it appeared from the picture you bore of it in your memory. Doubtless the scene had changed somewhat, but you yourself had also changed. It may have seemed less magical and more prosaic, yet you could bring to it a more mature appreciation of what it contributed to the being you had become.

In the individual life there is a gradual (graded) unfolding. The same applies to humanity as a whole. The consciousness of mankind is constantly changing. Each successive culture introduces new elements and provides the reincarnating human beings with new conditions in which to extend their awareness in new directions and on new levels. A brief historical background can give us a clearer perspective of how consciousness has constantly changed.

The first post-Atlantean cultural age was the Ancient Indian in Asia, characterized by an exalted spirituality. Human beings felt themselves to be more cosmic beings than earth dwellers. They had a memory of, and longed for, the instinctive, dreamlike clairvoyance of the previous Atlantean epoch. To them the spirit was real, whereas the external earthly world was an illusion, a deception, a mere appearance, from which they wanted to escape.

The following prehistorical Ancient Persian cultural age brought humanity a stage closer to the earth. The earth became a field of work, but the gaze was still directed to the heavens. The prevailing world-outlook can be called a spiritual chronology, using this term in the sense of the derivation of "logy" from *logos,* the divine creative Word. Thus chronology was no abstraction; it was the Logos of Time. This Logos of Time revealed Time as a living, superpersonal Being, ruling over a multiplicity of spiritual Beings of the cosmos which produce time. These included the twelve Amschaspands related to the signs of the zodiac, and the 28 to 31 Izeds who represented the daily changes of the Moon, regulating the days of the

7

month. The wonderful harmony of the cosmic order was maintained by the interweaving relationships in this Zarathustrian
world-picture of a living, spiritual chronology.

The third post-Atlantean cultural age was the Chaldean-
Babylonian-Assyrian-Egyptian, whose world-picture was a spiritual astrology, a Logos of the Stars, with a deeply spiritual basis.
The mysteries of the cosmos were transmitted not by intellectual
means, but by the instinctive sentient-soul activity that was conscious of the spiritual Beings of the stars. The grouping, motion,
and light of the stars in cosmic space was a divine stellar script. In
this script they discerned the laws of the cosmos and the will of the
heavenly Beings. Thereby they sought to harmonize earthly hap-
penings with what was taking place in the heavens.

The fourth cultural age, the Greco-Roman, was concerned with
meteorology, not as it is ordinarily conceived of today, but as revealing the Logos of the Atmosphere. The god for the physical Sun
was Helios, whereas the spiritual Sun was Apollo who worked in
the lively activity of the elemental spirits in the atmosphere, especially in the light, air, wind, vapor, and water. It was Apollo who
inspired and spoke through the unconscious soul forces of the
sibyls, particularly in the vapors giving rise to the prophecies and
wisdom proclaimed by the Pythia at Delphi. Apollo's harmonious
influence on the soul manifested through song and stringed instruments.

The meteorology of the Greeks brought them down toward the
earth into the realm of nature. They felt they belonged to munici-
palities, identifying themselves thus as Athenians, or as Spartans. A
Roman contribution to the fourth cultural age was people's awareness of themselves as individual human beings, as citizens of the
state possessing personal rights. Mankind had come a long way and
made a deep descent from the Ancient Indian cosmic consciousness alien to the earth, to the Roman consciousness of being
citizens on earth. In their art the Greeks objectified themselves in
material form, and they represented the gods after their own image.
It was in this age that the Christ incarnated on the earth: the divine
manifested as human in the physical world.

In the third age, the Chaldean-Egyptian, there arose another
cultural stream that continued on into the fourth age. This was the
Hebrew wisdom which can be designated as geology, the Logos of
the Earth. The Hebrews shut themselves off from what came from
the heavens. It was necessary for their world-picture that what

came from above should be opposed. All revelations had to come from the earth. Their deity, Jahve (Jehovah), was the ruler of the earth who chose to be a Moon-god to help the earth forward. As the Moon reflects the sunlight, so Jahve reflected the Christ-Sun forces.

According to Genesis, man was formed out of the forces of the earth and given an earth vesture. Adam means earth man, man of earth. Jahve, the ruler of the earth, breathed into him his own breath. Geology prevailed in Moses' revelation of Jahve—striking the rock, going up to the mountain, the pillar of fire connected with earth activity, the experiences in the desert. Unlike the Greeks who felt the forces that poured into the atmosphere from the surrounding cosmos, the Hebrews felt related to forces bound up with the earth.

This was in accord with the Hebrew mission which was to prepare a physical body, provide the earthly vessel, for the Incarnation of the Christ. No suitable body could have been prepared in the Ancient Indian, the Ancient Persian, or the Egyptian-Chaldean cultural ages. The full descent to the physical plane could not occur until the fourth, the central of the seven post-Atlantean ages, in the Hebrew stream dedicated to a spiritual geology, the Logos of the Earth. This stream had remained free from the exercise of unconscious soul forces used by other cultures. It appealed to the inner will in the keeping of the commandments, and to the clarity of the nascent ego exemplified by the Hebrew prophets.

After the successive ages of descending evolution, it was possible to say in the fourth cultural age that "The Word became flesh and dwelt among us" (John 1:14), in order that an ascent might begin, and that in the course of ages and epochs, the flesh might become the Word. In this very long process, what progress has been made in two millennia? Where do we stand today, a fourth of the way into the fifth cultural age which began early in the fifteenth century? What should be our world-picture now? A surface view of history may not be encouraging. Spiritually, much can occur without immediate external effects. Moreover, the human soul has had to mature to be ready for, and worthy of, deeper revelations, especially for an understanding of the deepest of all mysteries, the Mystery of Golgotha.

Through the Mystery of Golgotha the sublime cosmic Being, the Christ, having taken human form and experienced death and resurrection, permeated the aura of the earth. Thereby the earth was changed. Geology was christened, and Christ replaced Jahve as the new Lord of the Earth, yet he is at the same time "Lord of the heavenly forces on Earth." With rare exceptions this was not then understood, hence the expectation that an earthly kingdom would be established. During the Greco-Roman age the time was not ripe for, nor was human consciousness yet capable of grasping the connection between the earth and the cosmos. This aspect of the Christ-impulse can be likened to a stream that for some distance flowed underground.

Our present fifth cultural age is the time when it should surface. The central stage in every time cycle of seven is the fourth. The fifth, which begins the ascending arc, bears a relationship to the third. We have seen that in the third cultural age, the Chaldean-Egyptian, the world-picture was astrology, the Logos of the Stars. In our fifth age, there will arise the wisdom of the stars in a new form, for consciousness has changed; meanwhile the Christ has come to the earth, uniting the earth with the heavens in a new way. The world-picture that will more and more be recognized as the right one for our modern time is a *Christ-filled cosmology.*

The central stage is four in every cycle of seven

To date in our century, we have made stupendous achievements in outer space, radically changing our concepts of the earth's place in the cosmos. One writer proclaims that we have become a spacefaring people and "will never again be bound entirely to the cosmic frog pond of the earth," or, as others called it, "a mole hill in the universe," or "a speck of dust in the Milky Way."

On January 2, 1914, Rudolf Steiner explained that mankind had "first to seek for the connection of the earth with cosmic powers in the most external field, the field of the most external science." In the same lecture one finds, "it will be necessary to learn to read the stellar script again in a new form." The living essence, the soul and spirit of the world of the stars, and the spiritual activities of the stars must be recognized again. They were thus known by Johannes Kepler. He is honored for his astronomical laws, but few know that in him lived a Christ-filled cosmology, in which the earth and planets were seen as ensouled. Early in the seventeenth century this concept rose like a fountain briefly, then disappeared again underground.

In the twentieth century the stream has surfaced, appearing as a science of the spirit which reveals the individual as a spiritual being belonging to the whole cosmos. This is true in sleeping and waking, in all of life's unfolding from conception to death, and in the life between death and rebirth. It is the function of our cultural age to bring this to mankind's consciousness.

Each cultural age lasts 2,160 years, the same length of time it takes for the Sun, by precession of the equinox, to pass through one sign of the zodiac. However, the dates of the cultural ages do not coincide with the zodiacal dates. They extend from about the middle of a zodiacal age to the middle of the next one. Our present cultural age began in 1413 A.D. and will last until 3573, whereas the vernal equinox will move from Pisces to Aquarius around 2500 A.D. That is when the much-talked-of Aquarian Age will begin astronomically. The purer Aquarian influence will manifest in the middle of the sign, when the sixth cultural age will begin in 3573. The world-picture will then change again as will human consciousness. It will be an age of brotherhood, just as a Christ-filled cosmology characterizes our present fifth cultural age.

In addition to our cultural age causing a change in consciousness, there are two other rhythms which contribute to the marked change in the twentieth century. One is a much longer rhythm than that of the cultural age, for it lasted 5,000 years. In esotericism it is called the Dark Age, or Iron Age—Kali Yuga in the East. It began in 3101 B.C. and ended in 1899 A.D. During those 5,000 years humanity gradually lost conscious connection with the spiritual world. In 1900, the very threshold of the twentieth century, the Age of Light began. It will last 2,500 years and extend into the fifth millenium. It opens the door to the supersensible spheres, and leads humanity gradually out of the darkness of materialism into the light of the spirit.

The other rhythm is a much shorter one and is exceedingly important for us now. The instreaming of new impulses into human evolution during each period of about 350 years is fostered successively by seven Guiding Archangels connected with the Moon, the Sun, and the planets. Archangels are supersensible Beings two ranks above man, as man is two stages above the plant kingdom. As we do not see the wind, but observe its effects, so, although the

archangels themselves are not sense-perceptible, the effects of
their activity are evident.

Early in the sixteenth century, Gabriel, who directs the forces of
the Moon, became the Ruling Archangel. In 1879 the rulership was
taken over by Michael, Archangel of the Sun. No two planets differ
as much from each other as do the Moon and the Sun, hence no two
archangelic ages differ as radically as do those of Gabriel and
Michael. Some basic differences between them can be outlined
thus:

Gabriel Age	*Michael Age*
Materialistic science	Spiritual science
Brainbound intelligence	Spiritual intelligence
Fragmentation	Wholeness
Emphasis on heredity	Body, soul, and spirit
Nationalism	Cosmopolitanism
Religious sects galore	Unifying element active
Christ humanized or ignored	Cosmic Christianity

While fully recognizing that materialistic science is valid in its
own field, and while marveling at the tremendous triumphs it has
made, it is needful to recognize also that in this Michael Age there
has emerged a spiritual science. This science of the spirit is no
vague pantheism. It presents exact knowledge of supersensible
worlds and of how they interpenetrate the physical world.
Although the first century of the Michael Age (nearly a third) has
passed, Gabriel-Age characteristics, which served a good purpose
earlier, still persist one-sidedly and are now retarding instead of
promoting progress.

Throughout the ages—from the word-picture of chapter 12 of the
Revelation of St. John to innumerable paintings over the centuries—Michael has been portrayed as the Archangel who overcomes
the dragon. The connotation of the dragon has changed with changing consciousness. The picture that persisted until the eighteenth
century, the middle of the Gabriel Age, was that the lower instincts
in human beings had to be overcome by the higher forces.

In our Michael Age the dragon forces are those that would keep
people bound to the materialistic conceptions which had their
rightful place in the Gabriel Age, but which threaten humanity
with destruction if prolonged into the future. Instead of picturing
Michael in armor slaying the dragon, modern artists show Michael

as a shining sunlike Being from whose light the dark, bony figure of Ahriman retreats.

To speak of Ahriman and his hosts accords with supersensible reality. These are the forces of darkness which enslave human beings to earthly life, blind them to the spirit and to their spiritual relation to the cosmos. They drag mankind down to the sub-human level, unfree and machinelike. They feast on numbers, abstractions, standardization, and education without moral value, an education that makes one very clever, but leaves the soul empty. They subtly try to control the economy. They engender fragmentation, splits, hatred, fear, race riots, strikes, and irresponsibility. They inspire the get-all-I-can attitude, the antithesis of the Michael impulse to serve selflessly inspired by world-purpose.

Even in the pictures of Michael in armor, his countenance is calm and serene, free from any trace of hatred, passion, or conflict. He has a task to perform and does it with confidence, assured of victory. In the current Michael Age, however, we may well ask, Will he win? Will wholeness be restored to our fragmented culture? Each soul must answer for itself. Michael does not compel. He merely points the way to a new direction, a cosmic direction, for unlike any former ages, individuals now walk the new way *in freedom*. The impulses of the future no longer work automatically in human beings. Tremendous responsibility rests on humankind, for Michael allows full freedom.

> Michael points to a great change,
> Change that is cosmic in range.

In a material sense, people have responded enthusiastically and courageously to the impulse to explore the cosmos. In a spiritual sense, relatively few but growing numbers have an insight into cosmic spirituality and, more essentially, a comprehension of cosmic Christianity which Michael fosters. As the Archangel of the Sun forces, Michael is most deeply connected with the Christ, the sublime Being of the Sun who united himself with Earth evolution. The cosmic nature of the Christ was always known in the secret mystery places, even in pre-Christian times. Also since the Incarnation of the Christ in Jesus of Nazareth it was known wherever esoteric Christianity was cultivated. With the dawn of the Michael Age, this knowledge could be made public, and appear in a spiritual scientific form suitable for twentieth-century consciousness.

Christ himself said to his disciples: "I have yet many things to say unto you, but you cannot bear them now" (John 16:12). The greatest confidence, courage, and strength of soul can come from the new understanding of the Christ which is possible in this Michael Age, and from the appearance of the *Etheric* Christ from the twentieth century onwards. The dragon is active in thwarting this new understanding, and in promoting the expectation of a physical second coming of Christ. Whatever success has attended the dragon's efforts to reduce the concept of the Christ to that of a man, and to reduce man to an animal, helps to prevent the individual from finding his true ego and from assuming individual moral responsibility for every thought, word, and deed.

When we say "I," it includes everything within our consciousness. The Christ as the Cosmic "I" encompasses everything in the cosmos. It will take many incarnations and many future cycles of time for us to attain such comprehensiveness. We ascend in that direction when our world-picture is a Christ-filled cosmology and we consciously know ourselves to be *citizens of the cosmos.*

3

PLANETARY LAWS—THE KEY TO LIFE'S UNFOLDING

"THE world's next great step is not in the realm of science or materialism. It is in the Realm of SPIRIT, and the world will then make the greatest progress of all time." This statement was made not by a spiritual leader but by the eminent scientist Steinmetz (1865–1923). His as yet less-known contemporary, Rudolf Steiner (1861–1925), a spiritual scientist, did indeed make the great step into the realm of the spirit. However, mankind in general has not yet taken the step. In the intervening half-century, science has made tremendous advances, whereas there has been no comparable comprehension of the spirit in the world and in human beings. As a result of this omission, there is an increasing number of disturbed individuals and growing social disorder, now threatening even the progress of civilization itself.

The time has come to think not only in terms of natural laws, but also in accordance with planetary laws that affect us as threefold beings of body, soul, and spirit. By doing so, we attune ourselves consciously to cosmic rhythms and feel related to the cosmos as well as to our earthly environment. When we see the disorder man is creating, it is encouraging to know that order does exist in the cosmos. We can be sure that the sun will not rise a minute or even seconds late. In proportion to our recognition and application of the cosmic laws, order will be restored in individual lives and in earthly affairs.

Presented in this volume is the *key* whereby you can for yourself understand the planetary laws that govern life's unfolding from conception to death, and from death to rebirth. This will explain much that has happened and is happening in your own life. It should enable you also to have a better insight into the needs and struggles of people of all ages. It establishes, too, a closer kinship with all members of the human family—both on earth and in the supersensible spheres. No longer need one be an insecure, isolated, or proud individual. Without losing one's full worth as an ego

being, one humbly, reverently, and securely feels oneself united
with the cosmic whole.

In past ages this relationship was described as a microcosm within, and reflecting the macrocosm. Materialistic thinking split the
connection between the microcosm and macrocosm in human consciousness. When human beings lost their spiritual connection with
the heavens, they lost that part of themselves which made them
whole. Thereby each gained freedom and an awareness of his or
her own separate, independent I. To regain a whole view of the self
on a higher level enriched by the individual I-consciousness, people need to recognize once more that each is a microcosm in the
macrocosm. The microcosm cannot know itself without knowing
the macrocosm.

Our solar system encircled by the zodiac is our macrocosm. The
twelve signs of the zodiac have a fixed sequence. They relate to the
twelve parts of the physical body from the head (Aries) to the feet
(Pisces). The signs of the zodiac are no more interchangeable than
are the head and feet. These "twelve points of permanence" are the
dwelling places of sublime spiritual Beings who sustain and maintain our solar system and its relation to other systems.

Whereas the number twelve rules what is side by side in *space*,
the number seven has to do with what occurs in *time*. The planets
moving within the bounds of the fixed zodiac establish time se-
quences and relationships. As there is a correspondence between
the twelve signs of the zodiac and the twelvefold spatial physical
human form, so there is a correspondence between the moving
planetary pattern and life's unfolding in the course of time from
conception to death. In order to understand life's unfolding in the
microcosm, we need to understand the planetary pattern in the
macrocosm.

This pattern was described by Rudolf Steiner, a scientist of the
supersensible whose methods were as precise as those of the most
exacting natural scientist; hence he was called the "scientific seer."
In 1924 he summarized the planetary pattern thus: "Together with
the earth we exist within seven interpenetrating spheres and we
grow into them, enter into connection with them in the course of
life. Our life from birth to death is unfolded out of its original
inherent tendencies, inasmuch as the star spheres draw us from
birth to death. When we have reached the Saturn sphere we have
passed through all that the beings of the various planetary spheres
in grace accomplish for us, and then, speaking in the occult sense,

we enter into a free, moving cosmic existence of our own. It is an existence . . . that can, in a certain sense, be emancipated from what, in earlier life periods, are still necessities."[1]

Let us picture this planetary pattern specifically. From the physical point of view, the Sun is in the center of our planetary system. Orbiting around it are Mercury, Venus, the earth with its Moon, Mars, Jupiter, Saturn, Uranus, Neptune, and Pluto. From the point of view of the unfolding of an earthlife from birth to death, the earth becomes the center of activity. Using the earth instead of the Sun as the starting point, the order of the planets changes. The designation "planet" in this context includes the Sun and also the earth's satellite, the Moon.

The influence of a planet is not confined to the visible material planet we see in the sky. It extends throughout the entire sphere bounded by an orbit determined by a radius reaching from the earth to the planet. In this sense the earth is at all times within all the interpenetrating spheres, resembling the layers of an onion. The influence of each planet lasts for seven years, then the next in

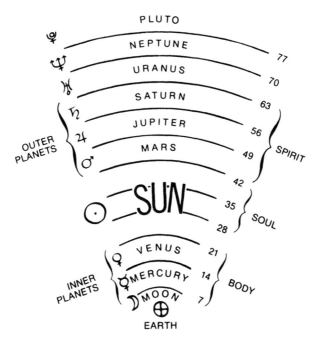

The planetary spheres ruling the stages of development

succession provides further unfolding. In the light of this presentation of the planetary spheres as spiritual realms, it is consistent to capitalize Moon and Sun.

Nearest to the earth is the Moon. It rules the first seven years from birth to the change of teeth. Between the earth and the Sun are Mercury and Venus, which together with the Moon constitute the three inner planets. (Note that the place of Mercury before Venus accords with the spiritual viewpoint rather than the spatial position. In the latter, Venus is nearer the earth. The placing of Mercury before Venus accords with the *time* of their sidereal revolutions: Mercury 88 days, and Venus 225 days.)

So influential is the Sun in our solar system and in life's unfolding that it rules three cycles of seven, that is the years between 21 and 42. The Sun is central between the three inner planets—Moon, Mercury, and Venus—and the three outer planets—Mars, Jupiter, and Saturn. Beyond Saturn are Uranus, Neptune, and Pluto, known as the transcendental planets.

Uranus, Neptune, and Pluto were once comets. They joined our system later and still manifest certain eccentricities. They are not considered along with the basic seven planets from the Moon to Saturn, which are responsible for the life cycles from birth to 63. Recall that Steiner spoke of entering, at 63, "a free, moving cosmic existence of our own . . . that can, in a certain sense, be emancipated from what in earlier life periods, are still necessities." Descriptions of these emancipated cycles follow in sequence after the chapter on Saturn.

For those who are not acquainted with the influences of the various planets, there is needed a key to their nature. Needed also is some comprehension of the various members of the human being. Here is a brief characterization that will be enriched as you study the successive cycles of life's unfolding.

The human being in his or her wholeness is threefold, consisting of body, soul, and spirit. These three correlate with development in the life cycles of the threefold grouping of the planets: respectively, the inner planets, the Sun, and the outer planets. For a being of soul and spirit to descend from worlds of soul and spirit and enter a physical body on earth requires tremendous adjustments—far, far more than when one moves from one location to another, that is, to a different environment. The soul and spirit are present from the beginning, but can only gradually manifest their powers. The bodily organism must slowly undergo changes throughout the inner

planetary cycles, from birth to 21, before it can be a suitable instrument for the ego working in the soul during the Sun cycles from 21
to 42, and then, together with the soul, be an instrument for the
spirit from 42 onward.

A more detailed study of a person reveals that each part of the
threefoldness is itself threefold. The visible physical body, by itself,
is only a corpse. To be living it must be animated by a life body,
also called the etheric body, or body of formative forces. Plants
likewise have a life body. It distinguishes them from the minerals,
giving them life and enabling them to grow and reproduce. What
differentiates both people and animals from plants is that they have
desires; they feel, move on their own volition, and have consciousness, because in addition to the physical body and etheric body,
they have a soul body, usually called the astral body.

Human beings, in addition, rise above the animal kingdom by
virtue of *SELF*-consciousness—the ability to say "I," to speak, to
think, and to stand upright. This is because of the individualized
ego which the animal lacks. During the three Sun cycles between
21 and 42, the ego works on the threefold soul: the sentient soul,
21–28; the intellectual soul, 28–35; and the spiritual soul, 35–42, as
explained in later chapters. The threefold spirit is still only germinal, but functions in the cycles of the outer planets in accord with
one's evolutionary development and one's unfolding from birth
to 42.

Life's unfolding involves a series of births, correlated with the
planetary cycles. Each seven-year period marks a new birth. What
is ordinarily called birth is only the birth of the physical body as it
separates from the protective maternal organism. The first life cycle
is influenced by the *Moon*. The Moon governs the laws of heredity
operating in the physical body into which the soul and spirit enter
at physical birth. From conception to seven, the nurturing forces of
the Moon promote growth. At first they work primarily through the
mother, and then through the home environment. The mother and
the home are associated with the Moon. The initial dreamlike, instinctive consciousness, and the impulse to imitate are gifts of "the
Queen of the Night," who shines by reflected light, without light of
her own. It is in this period of infancy throughout the Moon cycle
that the organs are given form. The last of all are the teeth, the
hardest substance in the body.

The change of teeth indicates that the molding of the physical
organism is completed. This marks the time of the second birth, the

birth of the individualized etheric body from out of the sheath of universal ether, comparable to the birth of the physical body from out of the maternal sheath at physical birth. The etheric formative forces that had been active in molding the organs are free to be used for learning during the *Mercury* cycle from 7 to 14. The teacher becomes the messenger (Hermes—Mercury) mediating between the child and the world. Learning is fostered by pictures, contrasts, and rhythms, as Mercury leads the incarnating human being through the wonderful world of childhood.

Puberty signals the third birth, that of the astral body, around the age of 14. Puberty begins the *Venus* cycle, the period of adolescence with all its problems and pleasures. Venus is appropriately associated with the newly awakened individualized forces of love, which can be degraded to an animal level or elevated to beautiful, angelic, universal love.

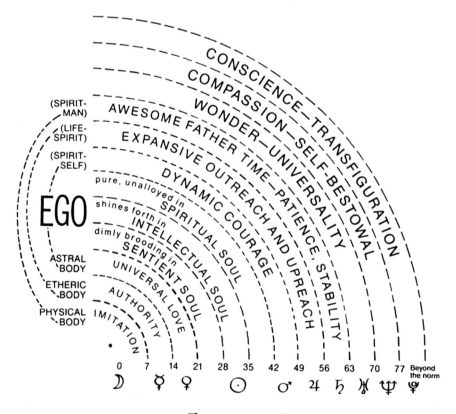

The seven-year cycles

☽   ☿   ♀   ☉   ♂   ♃   ♄

	☽	☿	♀	☉	♂	♃	♄
☽	0 ☽ 1	2	3	4	5	6	7
☿	7	8 ☿ 9	10	11	12	13	14
♀	14	15	16 ♀ 17	18	19	20	21
☉	21 22 23 24	25 26 27 28	28 29 30 31	32 33 34 35	35 36 37 38	39 40 41 42	
♂	42	43	44	45 46 ♂ 47	48	49	
♃	49	50	51	52 53	54 ♃ 55	56	
♄	56	57	58	59 60	61	62 ♄ 63	
♅	63	64	65	66 67	68	69	70
♆	70	71	72	73 74	75	76	77
♇	77	78	79	80 81	82	83	84

Annual planetary subdivisions

The ego organization is readied by 21, marking the fourth birth, the birth of the ego, upon entry into the first *Sun* cycle. By this time the bodily instrument has gone through all stages of its development. Thereafter, the changes every seven years occur in the soul and spirit. Therefore they are far subtler and outwardly less obvious, but nevertheless very potent inwardly throughout all the adult life cycles. The ego can undergo immense changes as it works on the threefold soul during the three Sun cycles from 21 to 42.

The negative nature of *Mars* manifests as aggression, conflict, warlike tendencies, and excessive passion, making 42–49 "the dangerous forties." In its positive nature Mars gives courage, dynamic energy, and constructive activity.

Jupiter, 49–56, strives toward outreach and upreach, again in a negative or positive sense. It promotes a more philosophical approach to life, giving rise to greater tolerance, a more "jovial" attitude, and optimistic outlook. Activity is motivated by wisdom.

Saturn, awesome "Father Time," brings a more serious mood from 56 to 63. In the lesser evolved individual, Saturn instills fear and isolation. In the more highly evolved, Saturn's influence is evident in deep concentration, calm stability, and stately maturity.

The unique contribution of this book is that it goes beyond the unfolding of the seven-year life cycles. It subdivides each seven-year period, allotting a year to each of the seven planets in the same sequence as in the larger seven-year ordering. The first of each seven is a Moon year; the second is a Mercury year; and the third is a Venus year. Thus the first three years are ruled by the three inner planets and confer to each life cycle what is comparable to infancy (Moon—a new beginning, adjustment, and growth), childhood (Mercury—learning), and adolescence (Venus—love and beauty).

The fourth, the central year of every seven, is always ruled by the Sun, which strengthens ego awareness and promotes ego activity. So mighty is the Sun's influence that it extends beyond a single year. It overlaps with the last two-thirds of the previous Venus year, and the first two-thirds of the following fifth year. This should always be kept in mind.

Note also that the demarcation between all years, and between the seven-year cycles, is not rigid. As between day and night there is twilight, so between all periods there is a flexible and gradual transition.

The fifth, sixth, and seventh years of every seven-year period are ruled by the outer planets: Mars (energetic activity), Jupiter (expansion), and Saturn (culmination, completion, stability, and maturity).

This gives the key to life's *year-by-year* unfolding as well as to the successive seven-year cycles of the entire earthlife.

We should actually retain the possibility, all through life, of rejoicing in the coming year, because each year charms forth the divine-spiritual content of our own inner being in ever new forms. I want to emphasize this point. We should really and truly learn to experience our life as capable of development not only in youth, but through its whole span between birth and death.[2]

PART I

Life's Unfolding from Conception to Death

4

EARTHLIFE BEGINS

THE FIRST YEAR: FROM CONCEPTION TO THREE MONTHS AFTER BIRTH

IN READING the title, "Life's Unfolding From Conception to Death," you may have wondered why "conception" was used instead of "birth." The choice was deliberate, and has special meaning in our time. For years, when studying Rudolf Steiner's lectures, I was always impressed by the fact that whenever he said, "Going back to birth," he invariably added the phrase, "or rather to conception." Since abortion was legalized, we see that there certainly was a need for calling our attention to the fact that life on earth begins at conception.

What happens at conception? The explanation of this can be understood only if we start with the third premise of the first introductory chapter, which regarded the individual as a being of soul and spirit as well as body. It related this being of body, soul, and spirit to the spirituality of the universe, and revealed that man has many lives on earth, between which are sojourns and sublime experiences in the cosmic spheres, as described in Part II of this book. If we start with this premise, we realize that as we journey down through the cosmos in preparing for a new birth, a spirit-germ of cosmic vastness is prepared, involving even the sphere of the zodiac, which provides forces for our physical form from our head to our feet, from Aries to Pisces. Created in the cosmos long before birth, this spirit-germ for the physical body gradually contracts and unites with the physical-germ provided by the parents at conception.

Speaking on the subject, "Is Abortion a Crime?," the Rev. John Hunter of the Christian Community made this significant point: "We speak about the mother-to-be. We should say that she is already a mother from the moment of conception." For already at conception the spirit-germ unites with the physical-germ. Within three weeks the etheric or life forces, and the higher members of man's being, which we call the astral body and the ego, are also lowered down.

Not immediately but in the course of the embryonic period, these supersensible bodies become active. During the first seven weeks the mother's etheric and astral bodies work on the embryo. At about the seventh week, the etheric body—the life forces, the formative forces—of the incoming ego start to be active. By the seventh month the child's astral body enters into the process. In the last part of the prenatal development, the ego is also at work, mediated by the mother's sheaths, and finally begins independent action at birth.

The trend today to natural childbirth, with the full consciousness and cooperation of the mother and father, and also the possibility of the birth occurring in the home, are wholesome. The experience is enhanced if a holy mood prevails. This can scarcely be possible if man is regarded as only the highest animal. When our thinking is no longer bound by the materialism of our age, when it advances to spiritual intelligence, we shall know with full certainty that our origin is divine. Verily, *Ex Deo Nascimur:* out of God we are born.

We human beings are born out of the divine. We have descended from spiritual heights. Between each death and new birth we pass through the cosmic worlds, and our entry into earth-existence is attended by angels, as an occasional sensitive doctor is aware. As sensitivity increases, it will be recognized that it is also important who first touches the child at birth and how it is handled. Fortunately, a renewed awareness of our spiritual home is reflected in the popularity and acceptance of Frederick LeBoyer's book, *Birth Without Violence,* which treats the infant not as a "thing" but as a spiritual being—a feeling entity to be received with love and respect.[1]

The taking of the first breath is an extremely significant moment. In addition to the air, there are inhaled and imprinted on the sensitive organism the cosmic forces which the incarnating ego chose as most appropriate for its unfolding life on earth. To interfere artificially with this chosen fulness of time is unthinkable to anyone cognizant of spiritual realities.

According to Rudolf Steiner: "A certain horoscope is allotted to a person because within it, those forces find expression which have led him into being . . . for the external world the true science of these matters has been for the most part completely lost." Also,

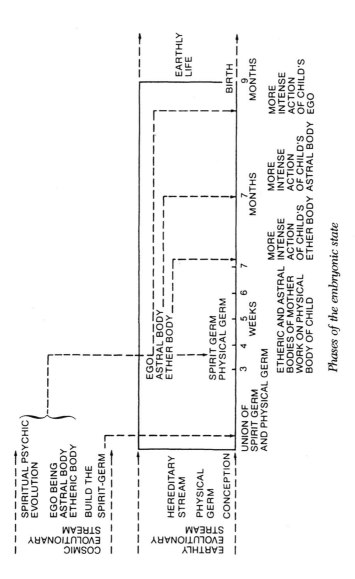

Phases of the embryonic state

Source: From *Reincarnation as a Phenomenon of Metamorphosis* by Guenther
Wachsmuth, Ph.D., Philosophic-Anthroposophic Press, Dornach, Switzerland,
1937, p. 161. Reprinted by permission.

"Man has within himself a picture of the heavens, and every man has a different one, according to whether he was born in this place or that, and at this or that time."[2]

The importance of the cosmic forces is again emphasized in this statement, "In the future mankind will learn again, not only to insure that a child shall have good milk to drink and good food to eat—although no objection is to be made to this—but mankind will learn again to observe whether this or that person has within him forces of Saturn or Jupiter active under this or that influence."[3]

When mankind becomes conscious that coming to birth is far more than a physical process, that it requires the cooperation of heavenly and earthly forces, then the unconscionable, brutal slaughter of millions of the unborn will cease. Conception and coming to birth will assume an aura of sacredness befitting these sublime cosmic-earthly events.

The Holy Birth, so beautifully described by St. Luke and portrayed by artists who still had supersensible vision or awareness, was indeed a unique event. It presents an ideal for every mother, an archetype of supreme purity, holiness, and selfless devotion and love. Rudolf Steiner recommended that during pregnancy and after giving birth, mothers meditate regularly on pictures of the Madonna, particularly Raphael's Sistine Madonna.

The Annunciation too is archetypal. In ancient times, especially among certain tribes in northern Europe who had a dim clairvoyance, there appeared to women who were to conceive a spiritual being who announced the coming child. Special human beings—for example, St. Francis of Assisi—have from time to time been announced to one or both parents. Prophetic annunciations and conscious connection with the incoming ego may occur increasingly as human consciousness is heightened.

In the embryonic period there is a communication between mother and child through the rhythmic beat of the mother's heart. This is the initial basis of language. It provides a vocabulary of sounds and distinct rhythmic patterns centering in the larynx of the embryo. At birth the child misses this, and needs rocking, cuddling, and the mother's voice, especially a soft singing voice, but no mechanical sounds as of radio or television.

Later language difficulties have been found among children whose mothers had heart disturbances during pregnancy. It is of interest that in the first three months there is a universal baby language with varied sounds found the world over. After the first three months this baby language is gradually transformed into the mother tongue.[4]

This three-month period after birth indicates that coming to birth is connected not only with the forces of the Moon, which are closely associated with reproduction, but also with the course of the Sun during the year.[5] The ten lunar months of the embryonic period are, of course, nine solar months. To these can be added the three months following birth, which in certain respects represent a continuation of embryonic life.

This realization, which can be affirmed by a perceptive faculty for observing the infant, should determine one's relation to and care of the baby. The transition from the warmth, the darkness, the soft waterbed, and the protective security of the mother's womb, to the external world's fluctuating temperature, light, air, noise, gravity, and separateness can be violent, painful, and damaging if there is little understanding of this change, and the needs of the infant. Recall how blinding it is to turn on a light in the middle of the night. It is even more disturbing to the infant, who has never experienced light, to be thrust at birth into a brightly lit room. No matter how hygienic and "scientific" the nurseries and maternity wards are kept, certain basic needs are usually not met. On the other hand, LeBoyer's book *Birth Without Violence* provides insight and a practical technique for minimizing the trauma of birth by taking into account the environment from which the infant emerges and that into which it is born.

Fortunate is the infant who can be kept with the mother, be breast-fed if possible, feel her nearness, and experience being enveloped in her soul love in an atmosphere with moderate light and stillness, devoid of mechanical interferences. During the embryonic period the mother's organism contains three times the normal amount of copper, because copper has connecting and protecting qualities. If from the moment of birth the infant is separated from the mother and not cuddled, the transition is a cruel one, even if done in ignorance. But, understanding is increasing, and even "experts" are learning the need for cuddling, which promotes physical and psychic health.

The needed connection between mother and child is beautifully portrayed in Raphael's madonnas, especially the Madonna of the Chair. They show an intimate relationship that has a spiritual reality. One feels that the mother and child belong together.

Gradually, with the growth and development of the infant, increasing freedom of movement is achieved. First, the head is raised independently, and by two or three months the infant may make efforts to raise itself. Then the "three-month continuation of embryonic life" is completed and the child is ready for further unfolding.

THE MOON CYCLE, 0–7—FROM BIRTH TO THE CHANGE OF TEETH

A mother, walking a few steps ahead of her three-year-old child, noticed too late that he had walked through a small pool of water in the sidewalk. Angrily she shouted at him, "You know better than to do that!" Had she struck him a physical blow it would not have hurt the child any more than did her verbal lashing. One could feel that the "space" between them widened. Little wonder, then, if that child becomes antisocial as he grows older and strikes out at the world around him.

In contrast, a middle-aged woman lovingly held her four-month-old godchild. In a hopeful tone she said, "I wonder what you will be when you grow up." Her faith was envisioning for him a radiant future. Held warmly in her aura, the infant was being impregnated with the service-ideal to which her life is dedicated.

Right care of children is one of the most urgent needs of our time. It should be undertaken wisely if we are to look forward to the future with hope, courage, and joy. For, much of the crime and destructiveness that arouse fear and alienation today had their rise in generations miseducated during the decades of materialism when man was considered the highest animal. In the 1930s, young parents I knew, both teachers in New York City schools, told their son's nursemaid to treat the two-year-old simply as an animal.

Through the 1970s, education was increasingly mechanized and relegated to television and teaching machines. This deprives children of living human contact and the worthy examples they need if they are to grow up not as machines or animals, but as men and women in the true sense of the words. I recall that when I was in elementary school early in this century, our minister's children once stayed with us a few days. The preschool boy gave us a surprising answer when he was asked what he wanted to be when he grew up. His instant reply was, "A man!"

Life from conception to death is a unity, a whole, although it unfolds in stages that differ markedly from one another. In life's unfolding we progress through the expanding spheres of the Moon,

Mercury, Venus, Sun, Mars, Jupiter, and Saturn in a rhythmic succession of seven-year cycles, allowing, however, three seven-year cycles for the Sun. As the nearest orb to the earth is its satellite the Moon, so the first stage of earthlife, the seven years from birth to the change of teeth, is under the influence of the Moon.

Each of the seven-year periods can be subdivided by designating a year for each planet, in the same order as for the seven-year cycles. Thus, the first year after birth is the Moon year of the Moon cycle, therefore doubly under the Moon's influence. We could then subdivide the year, making the first seventh, that is, fifty-two days, triply under the influence of the Moon. With the Moon, the Queen of the Night, we associate sleep and dreams. The infant sleeps most of the time in the early months, when the Moon forces are strongest.

If we really feel that the infant is a spiritual being newly come from spiritual heights, "trailing clouds of glory," as Wordsworth wrote, and that "heaven lies about us in our infancy," then our attitude toward the child will be one of great reverence, in fact, one might say the attitude of a priest. We realize that we are in the presence of something holy and sacred.

The process of a soul-spiritual being from the spiritual worlds incarnating and adapting to life on earth is very complicated and difficult, especially in our modern, materialistic times. Much damage is done unwittingly by subjecting the sensitive infant to noise, mechanization, and unspiritual attitudes. It is especially damaging to impose at too early an age learning processes that interfere with the basic task of preparing the organism to be a capable instrument in later life. The soul and spirit are present from the beginning, but before they can function in earthly life, their instrument, the body, must gradually be made ready.

From the nature of the Moon we can discover what is appropriate during the seven-year lunar influence. What light do we receive from the Moon? Nothing but reflected light received from the Sun, the planets, and the stars. What can we expect from the young child who does not yet have any soul activity or thought of his own? What is he? He is an imitator, reflecting his environment. And what is the Sun for this sensitive moon-reflector? The parents and the people surrounding him should be as a sun to him.

A little child is all sense-organ.[6] Have you observed how he reacts? Instead of merely smiling in response to a loving gesture, what does he do? He usually shakes all over, right down to his toes, for the body as a whole acts as a sense organ and responds to every impression. You may have observed that later, when he has learned to imitate movements, he imitates precisely. For example, if you wave one hand, he waves one hand; if you wave both hands he will do likewise.

But he does not imitate only gestures.[7] He takes in every thought and feeling in the environment; thus the mother cannot hide any emotional strain from the child.[8] His entire organism is like a sponge, absorbing all impressions into his bodily processes. All the inner feelings, thoughts, and moral impulses he absorbs from his environment are a molding force and are reflected in the whole organism of the child, conditioning his brain and his vascular and other systems for his entire earthlife. What he needs most are the right examples to reflect and to imitate. This imitative period lasts from birth to the change of teeth, at approximately the seventh year, which concludes the Moon cycle.

The Moon forces are those of growth. During the first seven years the physical body is in the process of growth, and the formative forces are shaping and developing the organs. The brain and all the organs receive their permanent formation—not their size, which will enlarge later—but their actual formation during the first seven years. Every feeling and thought absorbed from the environment contributes to this shaping process. This reveals the importance of right examples during these years, particularly in respect to the mother and the home environment. Both the mother and the home are ruled by the Moon. However, it should not be overlooked that fathers, who have the Moon-ruled sign Cancer dominant in their nativity are often more motherly than are many mothers.

Nothing which is worthy of being imitated should be imparted to the child except by example. To treat the child as a miniature adult, and prematurely expect learning for which his abilities are not yet organized, would be to injure him for life, just as an embryo would be injured by exposure to sunlight and air while it still needed the protective sheath of the mother. All of a child's formative forces are needed in building up the body until the time when the second teeth appear. The appearance of the second teeth is indication that the formative forces are released from the main task of molding and developing the various organs and are now free for learning activities. Thus the Moon cycle comprises the first seven years, the formative years, molding the body and promoting growth.

During the first three years of childhood, prior to conscious memory and out of a wisdom that far transcends ordinary consciousness, every normal human being receives three spiritual gifts: the ability to walk upright, to speak, and to think.[9] Whether or not we have children of our own, or grandchildren, or merely have contact with children in our environment, it is good for us as adults to realize that we were once children and received free from the spiritual world these three priceless gifts whose importance we are apt to forget or take for granted. And take them for granted we all too often do, unless we suffer from some impairment which deprives us of their normal use. Stubbing a toe or a touch of laryngitis may make us painfully aware of the value of the gifts of walking and speaking.

Animals such as a chick, a calf, and a colt can walk from birth, whereas human beings must gradually learn to lift their heads to the light, must acquire the ability to free themselves from gravity, and learn to stand and walk in an upright position. By six months of age most children can sit without support, and some can crawl; by the first birthday they can take their first steps.[10]

Likewise in the ability to speak, man differs from animals. When the first breath is taken at birth, human expression begins with the first cry. There are universal babblings in the early months, then syllables, until early in the second year, the Mercury subdivision of the seven-year Moon cycle, there is a seemingly meaningless imitation of sounds. By the eighteenth month there is meaningful response and "naming"—connecting things with names—that represents a passing from expression to speech. This stage in speech in the middle of the second year is comparable to the stage in bodily movement of sitting up in the middle of the first year. By the end of the second year, naming gives way to talking, an achievement comparable with walking at the end of the first year.

Thinking, the third gift of childhood, manifests next. Karl König says, "In the child's third year it is really as if the sun of thinking were to appear above the horizon and brightly illuminate the relations that have been formed between all his experiences."[11] This forming of relationships through thinking gives this subyear its Venus quality.

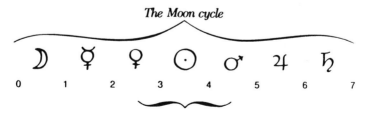

The Moon cycle

The child with the three gifts of walking, speaking, and thinking is then ready for a most significant, magical moment which occurs around the age of three. For the first time the child names its own self as only it, and no other being, can. Egohood dawns, and the child says, "I."[12] With this new ego-sense the child is able to perceive the ego of other human beings. The ego relates to the Sun forces, active in this central year of the seven-year cycle, even as the Sun is the central orb of our solar system. However, in this Moon cycle, the child experiences only a reflection or mirroring of the true "I." This fact is important. It is also important to note that as the Sun outshines all planets, its influence extends beyond the central year. It extends before the age of three and after the age of four, even as much as two-thirds of the preceding Venus year and the following Mars year. For this reason, some children start to say "I" soon after they are two years of age. The conscious memory begins with the dawn of the I-consciousness.

The awakening consciousness of oneself with the birth of the lower ego often sets up some defiance. I vividly recall one instance when a mother called in my husband and me when she could not manage her little girl at bedtime. It took the combined strength of both of us finally to overcome her herculean might.

Obstinacy may still be evident in the fifth year, the Mars subyear. In the Mars and Jupiter subyears, the young walking, talking, thinking ego-being courageously explores the expanding world around it. A friend told me she remembers distinctly that when she was five she and a playmate, who had ridden their tricycles only in front of their building, quite naturally ventured forth around the block. The child is first mature enough for moral understanding and for comprehending the meaning of "ought" after the age of five, because the will forces are freer from the physical organism than before that age. The child is more susceptible to guidance, and to obeying suggestions he or she has grasped.[13]

The forming of the bodily organism continues and reaches its climax and completion in the seventh year, the Saturn subyear, by pushing forth the most solid structures we have, the second teeth, ruled by Saturn. The formative etheric forces, having finished their seven-year task of body-building and growth, are then and only then available for learning.

Life's unfolding should be allowed to take place harmoniously in accordance with a natural, unforced tempo. The ill results of interference with this tempo are not usually apparent immediately, or even in a short time. Damage done in early years may manifest itself much later in life, for the latter years of life are often a reflection of the earlier years.[14] Some interesting correlations which Rudolf Steiner and others have revealed are the following:

Baby talk may result in weak digestion in later life.[15] Forced sitting and walking may lead to arthritis, as can also overloading the memory.[16] Premature standing, walking, memory exercises, and a general tearing of thinking away from feeling are among the causes of arteriosclerosis. Love and anger in the presence of a child affect the circulation, the good or ill results lasting throughout life. Natural truthfulness is lost if from ages one to seven the child sees a wholly falsified world. The worst that materialism can do is to ruin the whole of childhood so that the human being becomes incapable of taking in moral or spiritual impulses.[17]

A common error is to encourage or even permit a child to write and reckon by the age of five. A child-care center I pass daily has strung up on the wall the letters of the alphabet in capitals eight inches high. This is a sure way to kill the imagination and artistic feelings, and lead eventually to boredom. This applies also to abstractly constructed, ready-made toys which leave no room for fancy.[18] The much acclaimed and praised children's television program, "Sesame Street," might more appropriately be called "Disaster Street." Apart from the ruinous effect of being confronted by the rapid succession of bombarding, mechanical impressions, sounds, and pictures detached from the human soul and ego—thus paralyzing the sense for perceiving the ego of others—there is the disastrous damage of trying to awaken faculties and skills prematurely, long before the growing organism has become an instrument for them. Such "head starts" are more nonsensical than expecting blossoms from a seedling.

There is much to learn, too, about vaccination.[19] For one thing, it thwarts the useful purpose of childhood diseases. The physical body we inherit from the parents we chose never perfectly fits our individual destiny needs. The effort the organism puts forth to overcome the childhood disease results in reshaping the body more to our own heart's desire. Vaccination prevents that adaptation from taking place in a natural way. Furthermore, the vaccine is introduced at an arbitrary time when the organism is less capable of coping with it for its harmonious development. And, being injected directly, without the digestive processes acting on it to make it suitable for the body's use, as is done with food (milk), an alien element is introduced. The intense reaction of the organism to the foreign substance is detrimental. Sometimes the bad effects occur soon afterwards, but most often later in life. Animal-derived vaccines also cause a coarsening of the organs; and there is an inner connection between this early coarsening and a later materialistic outlook.

A pioneer in an anthroposophical approach to child care who works in Australia believes that "there is more to life than what is offered by the materialistic outlook of our age." After she retired from the state's child care service, she set up, in February 1976, a private consultancy which she called the Gabriel Baby Centre. (Gabriel is the Archangel connected with the Moon.) Less than a year later she wrote: "The care of infants is becoming more and more dehumanized in a number of areas—for example, commercially prepared foods, feeding babies meat broths at about 4 months of age, exercising the child artificially from a few weeks old onwards during the first year, the early teaching of reading and so on. It is a frightening spectacle! However, I have been greatly encouraged by the response I have received to the Gabriel work, and it is apparent that a number of young mothers are actively seeking a more meaningful way to bring up their children." On the completion of her fourth year her report is, "I had a busy 1979, and am glad to say that the Gabriel work is steadily growing."

A mother of two young children shared her view of parenthood: "Being a parent is such an incredible learning experience! It is wonder-full when taken seriously, but I often see examples of people who don't see the gravity of their task, and I hope and pray that the result won't be too devastating."

There is something in the soul and spirit of the human being that is marvelously latent and enduringly present, even when buried under deep layers of materialism and errors resulting from wrong upbringing. Strong, sturdy souls not only survive but develop added strength in counteracting adversities and handicaps produced in early childhood. They have the fortitude and wisdom to bear contentedly, without resentment or complaint, whatever infirmities they may encounter as a consequence of misguided early treatment.

Glorious connections exist between childhood and later life, but the pitfalls have been highlighted here in the hope that by being conscious of them, they may be avoided. Children must be allowed to be children, so that later they may experience a healthier and happier adult life. Inherent in a child's nature is a beautiful sense of reverence, especially in the presence of grownups. If this is allowed to flourish and is fostered, in time it becomes transformed. In later life it manifests as the power to inspire others, and is evident in the tone of the voice. And "one who has prayed in his childhood, can bless in his old age."[20]

5

THE MERCURY CYCLE, 7–14—FROM THE CHANGE OF TEETH TO PUBERTY

BEFORE an architect designs and erects a building, he or she needs to know the purpose for which the building will be used. The construction will differ if it is to be a house, an office building, or a church. Educational procedures are based on the educator's concept of the nature of the human being in general, and the developing child in particular. Educators who regard children as empty vessels or as mini-adults will educate differently from those who have a comprehensive knowledge of the whole human being consisting of body, soul, and spirit—the body having been designed by divine Beings to be the temple for the soul and spirit during a given incarnation.

Education has suffered immensely from the prevailing lack of this comprehensive knowledge. Although science has revealed much about the physical body, it usually either denies or disregards the soul and spirit. Only in such a barren climate could behaviorism arise and receive acceptance. Children are not empty vessels into which to pour knowledge, the earlier the better.

"If we were to continue our present way of living, when between the ages of 7 and 14 we are crammed with knowledge of every kind—there is of course a good side to this as well—we should gradually all suffer from something that was previously quite unknown and is now so prevalent—we should all suffer from 'nerves' as the saying goes, from nerve derangement."[1] In 1922 Rudolf Steiner gave this advice to teachers: "Don't think that you should pour this or that into the soul of the child. What you should do is feel reverence for its spirit. You cannot develop this spirit; this spirit develops itself. But your task is to remove all hindrances from its development and bring that which will stimulate it to develop itself."

Whether one is an architect or not, the obvious facts are that only at a specified stage can the wiring be installed, and that the building must be completed before it is equipped with furniture and occupied. Our civilization has developed amazing precision in machines and in programing, while overlooking the fact that timing is a very important factor in life's unfolding. It is a strange phenomenon of our time that although the adult life-span has been lengthened, the span of childhood has been shortened. We irreparably damage children if we treat them like miniature adults capable of a maturity they do not possess. I have a full-page advertisement picturing a small child in a library, reaching up to books on the fifth shelf above the floor. The caption beside it in big letters is: "At 4½ she's reading 3rd grade books." Also, "A child prodigy? not at all! your child, too, can be reading one, two or three years beyond his present age level."

Another full-page advertisement, bearing the Good Housekeeping seal, is headed, "Let the magic of reading begin years before first grade!" In fine print it states: "What fun to be able to read books ALL BY YOURSELF—when you're only three (or perhaps just two-and-a-half)! Lots of little kids are doing it these days. . . ." As we have said, this is as harmful to the child's well-being and right development as it would be to an embryo to expose it to light and air at three or four months, and to subject it to gravity instead of allowing it to float in fluid, free from gravity.

Spiritual sight reveals, and sensitive observation can confirm, that the incarnating human being experiences manifold births in its life's unfolding. As was explained in the introductory chapter on planetary laws, every seven years after physical birth a supersensible aspect of the indivdual's being is "born" and released for increased activity and maturing. These births are not accidental or chaotic. They follow planetary laws, bringing the seven-year cycles under the successive rulership of these seven planetary spheres: the three inner planets, Moon, Mercury, Venus; the central Sun (three-times seven years); and the three outer planets, Mars, Jupiter, Saturn. Once one is familiar with their order and functioning, one has the *key* to understand life's glorious unfolding. This key was already used in describing the nature of the Moon cycle from birth to the change of teeth, and its seven annual subdivisions.

The second period of seven years, the *Mercury* cycle, covers the time between two significant events, the change of teeth and puberty. These are the physical manifestations of the "birth" of the etheric body at seven, and of the astral body at fourteen. As the maternal sheath surrounds the embryo before physical birth, so an etheric sheath surrounds the child until seven. And as at its birth the physical body becomes independent of the mother, so the individual etheric or life body becomes independent of the universal etheric envelope at seven. Until this time, the formative life forces work on the inherited model, molding the organs. This activity on the physical organism is completed when the second teeth have been formed. By this time, not only have the first teeth been cast off, but the substance of the whole organism has been replaced, a fact recognized by science. Whether the inherited model is perpetuated or transformed in this process depends on factors in the environment, but most of all on the weakness or strength of the incarnating ego.

At seven the function of the etheric body changes from an essentially physical to a *soul* nature. It is injurious for the entire future life to tax the memory, to introduce reading and intellectual concepts, and to subject the child to mechanical impressions during the physically formative years before seven. After seven the individual etheric body is born, and is free for soul activity.

Mercury, or Hermes, the messenger

Authority in the Mercury cycle

In the Moon cycle, the entire body is a sense organ imitating all impressions received from its surroundings, centered primarily in the home and around the mother, both of them Moon influences. In the Mercury cycle, the surroundings widen more to the world beyond the home. There is need for an adult outside the family to be the guide in developing the awakening learning faculties, and to be the *interpreter* of the world to the soul of the child. Mercury, Hermes, messenger of the gods, is the apt symbol for this second seven-year cycle of life's unfolding.

Imitation and example are the magic words in education in the first seven years, the Moon cycle. What are they in the second, the Mercury cycle? Many persons will be surprised at the answer which Rudolf Steiner gives: *authority* and discipleship. They are the reverse of what has been practiced for many decades. A great tragedy in education in our century is the miseducation resulting from permissiveness, allowing children to do what they want to do and to make judgments at an age-period when they still need guidance and reverence for authority. If children do not have reverence for authority, they often grow up to be dictators. They are used to having their own way, so when they grow up they insist on the same attitude, and instead of meeting others on an equal basis, they want always to be at the head of things. These years can thus become the seedbed for breeding egotists. There cannot be true equality in later life if there has not been authority of the right kind, respected authority, during the ages of 7 to 14.

It is essential that the authority be nothing authoritarian, not militaristic, policing, demanding, or commanding. Reverence and veneration for a respected, naturally accepted authority will build the inclinations, attitudes, habits, and temperament which are required to develop the etheric body rightly during the Mercury cycle. The etheric body remains stunted if reverence and life-giving forces are lacking. Hence, the mood and the method are vitally important and should truly be life-giving for the etheric or life body. Life is needed to impart life. In the presence of a revered teacher who personifies life, enthusiasm, and love, an atmosphere is created that can never be duplicated by the most skillfully devised machines. Something invisible weaves between that teacher and pupils which nourishes their souls and continues to be a life-giving element in later life.

The recent introduction of teaching machines and open classrooms, in addition to the already prevailing emphasis on scientific training, have a hardening and deadening rather than a life-giving effect on the growing child. A friend who had a daughter in such a school system was deeply concerned about the shattering effect it produced. When the child, a willing and good pupil, returned home after the nerve-wracking day at school, it took some time for her to become normally tranquil. The only alternative was to send her to a parochial school. This, too, was unsatisfactory, because the private school sought to outdo the public school in making the pupils more scientifically intellectual.

The Mercury cycle is a time of learning by means of pictures, not by intellectual concepts. In the previous Moon cycle, the infant lived first in a sleeping state leading to an ever-increasing consciousness of the sense perceptions of the outer world. The whole body served as a sense organ. With the dawn of the seven-year Mercury cycle, the etheric forces have merely to maintain, instead of to mold, the physical organism. The released life body can devote itself to forming inner pictures not associated with external objects. Words and ideas should convey a meaning that is pictorial and artistic, not intellectual and scientific.

How health-giving these living pictures are in contrast to the passively observed, mechanically produced images flashing on a television or movie screen, or even in camera photos! They are created inwardly by the soul, exercising its innate artistic qualities and feeling forces, not just the head forces. Extremely important are these school years. Only the right methods based on a knowledge of the unfolding of the human being of body, soul, and spirit can prevent continued injury to our rising generation and generations to come, and thus restore health (wholeness) to humanity. To this end it is needful that the fragmented separateness, so prevalent, be replaced by the wondrous pictures and image-thinking which the child, with the guidance of the teacher, creates out of the living, integrated wholeness of the world and his or her place in it.

Physiologically, between the change of teeth and puberty, the rhythmic system becomes especially active. Therefore the role of the rhythm of breathing and blood circulation is most important. This indicates where the emphasis in education should be. Certainly not on the head in preoccupation with intellectual concepts, abstractions, and scientific facts, but on the feeling realm, involving movement and creative artistic activity. These activities include music, painting, modeling, fairy tales, legends, and pictures of the living earth organism and of the wisdom of the world. Most of the teaching in the lower grades should be given in life-filled stories which creatively motivate the children to produce the pictures within their souls. These nourish and fill the soul with treasures that enrich and enliven the entire life as it unfolds in later years. Many memory pictures will be understood intellectually only later.

Mercury is a planet that deals with dualities, with contrasts, and with alternating rhythms. The child soul delights in experiencing contrasting rhythms such as day and night, sunshine and rain, the seasons, and the festivals of the year. Contrasts and alternations increase the flexibility, mobility, and adaptability of the soul.

During the Mercury subyear of the seven-year Moon cycle—that is, during the second year—the child, quite instinctively and by imitation, learned to speak. Now in the seven-year Mercury cycle, 7 to 14, Mercury forces play an important part in helping the child consciously to master the written as well as the spoken word. This is the time to develop the arts of speaking, listening, and writing. In the Steiner or Waldorf Schools, the children learn writing before reading. This accords with the need for soul activity engaging not just the brain but the whole human being. The teacher who is inventive and has imagination can tell a story, for example, about a fish, and then have the children draw or paint a fish vertically. This can then be metamorphosed into the letter "f." Similarly, a mouth can be drawn for "m." In drawing, the hand and the will participate. And if the forms of the letters are "run" on the floor, the whole body is brought into movement. The letters of the alphabet are thus learned pictorially in a living way, not as abstract symbols. After this, reading will follow easily.

The seven planetary subdivisions and their age correspondences from 7 to 14 can be divided into three parts: the inner planets,

Moon, Mercury, and Venus, ages 7, 8, 9; the Sun, which is always central, age 10; and the outer planets, Mars, Jupiter, and Saturn, 11, 12, 13. The inner planets—especially the Moon, the first subyear—incline somewhat to carry over into the Mercury cycle the imitative quality of the previous Moon cycle. The outer planets foreshadow the intellectual powers that mature after puberty, which marks the birth of the child's own individual, independent astral body. Between these two groupings is the crucial sun year from 10 to 11, when there is the first astral quickening.

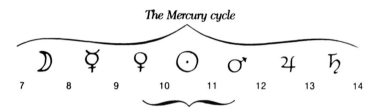

The Mercury cycle

Before this quickening, the teacher may be likened to a gardener tending children resembling plants. After this time, the teacher, from having been a gardener, now becomes somewhat of an animal trainer. The crisis for the teacher comes around the child's eleventh year, or between 9 and 11, when the teacher's authority is questioned. Previously the child felt one with the whole world, regarding everything as a unity. But as the Sun subyear approaches, self-consciousness awakens and the child feels more self-contained.

It was at the age of 3 (or 2⅓) to 4, the Sun subyear of the previous Moon cycle, that the first consciousness of the "I" dawned. At that time it was experienced less directly, as if reflected by the Moon. Now with the ego awakening in the sun subyear of the Mercury cycle, the child feels its self as differentiated from its environment. No longer do children feel that the outside world is a continuation of themselves as they did earlier when they still lived in a magical world. Now that the external world no longer belongs to the child's "I," the consequent sensation of aloneness contains the potential of loneliness, and perhaps even rebellion. In this mood the child begins to doubt the authority of the teacher.

This is indeed a crucial time, then, for without belief in the teacher's authority the child's inner security is lost. The teacher now needs to show the greatest sincerity and warmth of heart. The crisis at this age was illustrated in an article in the January 1975 issue of the *American Journal of Nursing*. It contained a description of the maladaptive behavior of a group of six boys, age 9 to 11, all in the fourth grade, and the work of a therapist in helping them.

In the light of the broader development indicated by the threefold grouping during the Mercury cycle, let us picture how the child unfolds year by year, and the appropriate approach in the art of teaching in these grade school years.

First, however, it must be emphasized that although the general pattern holds true, there must be flexibility in the age correlations. There is no rigid line of demarcation from one age to another. Just as day does not follow night without the transition of dawn, so from year to year and cycle to cycle there are transitions.

Ideally, we can say that the Moon year, 7 to 8, is the time to begin the first grade. Yet in practice, most children start the first grade when they are 6, that is, in their seventh year. Many turn seven in the course of the school year. Flexibility of attitude is always desirable.

In what follows, the subjects mentioned as appropriate for the given ages are far from complete. Only representative subjects are selected to illustrate the planetary correspondences as life unfolds.

The Moon, 7 to 8

In the first subyear ruled by the Moon, fairy tales delight the children and reveal the world as they see it, a magical world. The fairy tales also provide material for songs, plays, for learning the letters of the alphabet, counting, dialogues, and correcting wrong-doing.

Mercury, 8 to 9

Fables and legends can be added in the Mercury subyear of the Mercury cycle. Since the child does not yet distinguish between the living and the lifeless, it is proper that plants and animals, and even stones speak and manifest human qualities. In imaginative pictures, higher truths are expressed and the child grasps the inner reality in a way that enlivens and harmonizes the soul, whereas intellectual concepts dry up the soul. Stories about saints who mastered the animal weaknesses, and about heroic men and women, develop feeling in the right way and link the will with spiritual powers essential for a healthy character.

Stories that express polarization are also beneficial. Mercury deals deftly with dualities, with opposites, such as joy and sorrow, pleasure and pain, good and bad, beautiful and ugly. The child who, by emulating a worthy authority and by exemplary pictures of life, feels that the good is beautiful, has developed a sound moral sense.

Venus, 9 to 10

The Venus subyear comes when the child is beginning to lose his feeling of unity with the world. It is an appropriate time to use Old Testament stories picturing man's journey from paradise to the earth. One means of promoting social consciousness, which comes under the influence of Venus, is to practice writing letters. It is helpful to have a teacher who follows a class through all the grades and can now relate more individually with each child. The parents too should know the importance of giving extra understanding, love, and support to the child approaching age 10, when the danger of alienation is setting in.

Sun, 10 (9⅓–11⅔)

As the Sun outshines all the planets, so the Sun subdivision in any seven-year cycle may extend beyond one year, beginning earlier and continuing beyond it. The Sun year of the Mercury cycle can accurately be designated as covering the period from about nine and one-third to about eleven and two-thirds. There is always a transitional stage with no rigid time limits. Emerging from the subyears of the inner planets, Moon, Mercury, and Venus, and entering the Sun period is comparable to coming out of a protective cocoon. The child feels an increasing independence and detachment from the outer world with which he formerly was instinctively united, and now needs guidance and wise direction in uniting consciously with external nature and with the nature of man in a warm and meaningful way.

This requires that biology be presented, not in the soulless and spiritless fashion of natural science, but in a way that enables the child to feel that the whole world is a greatly differentiated living organism, and that he or she belongs to it. In botany, plants cannot be understood as separate entities, any more than can a hair apart from the body on which it grows. Plants grow with the help of the cosmos and the earth. They respond to the warmth and light of the sun, and to the soil, water, and air of the earth. The child should feel how the right soil is needed for the various plants; how the air and water work more on the leaves, light on the blossoms, and warmth on the fruit. The child should experience this living picture through feeling as well as knowledge. A picture of the refinement, purity, and innocence of plants and their offering themselves to the Sun produces a moral effect without speaking of morals.

During this Sun-ruled subyear of the Mercury cycle, the first astral quickening signals that the child is ready for a study of the animal kingdom. From the child's tenth to twelfth year, animals should be pictured in their relation to man, just as plants are shown as being related to the earth. Each animal species is an outer expression of its inner nature, of a definite soul quality. For example, we ascribe courage and majesty to the lion, and patience to the sheep. Animals display a variety of soul qualities, all of which can be found in some measure in people. However, "Man is the harmonious flowing together, or the synthesis of all the different soul qualities that the animal possesses. Man reaches his goal if in the whole being he has the proper dose of lion-ness, sheep-ness, tigerness, donkey-ness and so on; if all this is present in his nature in the right proportion and has the right relationship to everything else."[2]

How very important it is, when the child begins to feel separateness and alienation from the world, to be presented such a picture of wholeness! "Whole" is related to the words hale and health. Health of body, soul, and spirit is engendered when the whole human being is engaged in an artistic comprehension of the aliveness and interrelatedness of the whole world organism. The intellect engages only the head, and in our materialistic and intellectual age it has split, fragmented, disintegrated, isolated, and specialized life. No wonder there are increasing breakdowns, neuroses, destructive deeds, conflicts, strikes, and social chaos.

In Steiner education the principle of wholeness is applied to all teaching, even to arithmetic. It is deemed essential to learn division first, that is, to start with the whole and to divide it, rather than to add separate parts to make a whole. Division also stimulates greater flexibility. In adding, there can be only one answer, whereas in division twelve apples can be divided in many ways: 6 and 6, 5 and 7, 4 and 8, or 4 and 4 and 4, etc. Fractions in arithmetic, and grammar in language study, are not introduced until age 10.

The principle of wholeness is also applied to the organizing of the school day. In the morning there is a main lesson for two hours in one subject, studied consecutively for several weeks (no splitting of the time into short periods of mixed studies). Following the main lesson is group study, as in foreign languages; then arts and crafts, using the hands; finally eurythmy and physical education.

Mars, 11 to 12, especially nearest 12

A second quickening of the astral body and the dynamism of
Mars may result in a definite struggle between the personality of
the child and his teachers and parents. Unconsciously he wants the
teacher to be stronger, but outwardly he shows a contrary or even
combative spirit. It is important that the teacher prove his authority,
not as a dictator, but as a bridler of wild horses. Only thus can he
maintain his power of guidance.

Mars, as the first of the outer planets, brings about a change in
muscular functioning. Heretofore the muscles were related more to
the rhythmic system; hence music and art promoted their proper
growth. Now they relate more to the bone system and serve the
dynamics of the skeleton. The limbs tend to become lanky and the
mind more awake, and possibly critical. The child is now more
fully on the earth plane.

Until this occurs, it is premature and damaging to both body and
soul to teach the laws of the mineral kingdom. The method as
formerly should be to proceed from the whole to the part, and to
keep the connection with the living earth. Only between the
eleventh and twelfth years are children ready to distinguish between the living and the lifeless, and to be introduced to the laws of
cause and effect. Then physics and chemistry can be introduced,
based on observations from life. Appropriate at this age are Roman
history, and even geometry. Geometry can be made intensely interesting if the child experiences space through movement, and
sees that in nature "God geometrizes." Now, not earlier, a transformation of thinking can be safely undertaken. There can be a
gradual transition from a pictorial to conceptual form, in readiness
for abstract thinking later. If thinking till now has been pictorial
and living, the new conceptual thinking will be mobile and warm,
not rigid, coldly intellectual, and critical.

Jupiter, 12 to 13

Jupiter develops a more logical and intellectual approach in the
continuance of earlier studies, such as theory in science. Physiology and hygiene can also become a part of the curriculum. Medieval
and Renaissance history, highlighting great adventurers and dis-
coverers, fully accords with the spirit of Jupiter, as does further
exploration of the world around and the world within. Astronomy is
added as a main-lesson subject. It extends the sense of space to
world space and cosmic relationships.

Saturn, 13 to 14

Saturn rules the skeleton, hence physiology dealing with the skeleton is timely. There is a differentiation between spherical bones revealing cosmic forces, and elongated bones in which the earthly forces are more active. By comparing the predominance of the cosmic over the earthly in man, and vice versa in animals, a picture is presented of the dignity of man.

At this time historical studies should include the modern Industrial Revolution, with serious thought on its political and economic implications and the resulting social conditions. In mathematics, the wonders of algebra are open to exploration and lead to some abstract thinking. Excellent activity is provided by drama, and some of the less profound Shakespeare plays, particularly the comedies, can be acted at this age.

With the onset of puberty, the indrawing of the astral body reaches the reproductive organs, and strong inner desires develop. Parallel with it, there should occur an increase in reverence and amazement at the wonders of the world.

Mercury-Hermes bears the caduceus, the symbol of the healing art. The rhythmic system plays the largest role in the Mercury cycle, 7–14, and has much to do with health. It is an interesting fact that during these years the mortality rate is less than in the previous and following cycles. The breathing and heartbeat never cease and never tire, whereas activities of the head and the limbs do make us tired. Therefore, education during the Mercury cycle should focus as little as possible on head learning, and should involve the feelings and the heart in creative artistic activity.

In *The Little Prince* by Saint Exupery, the tamed fox teaches the little prince an important lesson: "It is only with the heart that one can see rightly; what is essential is invisible to the eye." The transition to adolescence will present many problems to those who approach puberty with the head and bypass the heart. Such souls are starved, lacking respect and love for the world around them, and lacking incentive and strength to control their instincts. Fortunate are those who formed pictures of the livingness of the world-organism, for they richly nourished and filled their hearts and souls during the Mercury cycle, "the heart of childhood."

6

THE VENUS CYCLE, 14–21—FROM PUBERTY TO THE COMING OF AGE

WHEN automobiles of certain models are faultily constructed and fail to function properly, they are recalled by the manufacturer for correction. However, when children are wrongly educated, the results are not always noticeable at once, and sometimes not until a whole decade or generation later. Unlike cars, they cannot be recalled to infancy in the home, or to childhood in the schools for correction.

Everyone is aware that teenage maladjustment, rebellion, belligerence, illegitimate births, and crimes have rapidly increased. The facts show that great social problems have not only been created for the present and the future, but also that basic preteenage training has been remiss and needs correcting.

Correction cannot be expected from parents and educators who themselves need correction, regarding both the true nature of the child and how life unfolds from year to year and from seven-year stage to seven-year stage. For example, a teacher asked a six-year-old child to report on three types of television programs for one assignment! Much in such education, although considered wholesome and praiseworthy, is yielding an undesirable harvest.

One of the foremost recognized problems today is the energy crisis. Another that far eclipses it in importance, yet is little recognized, is the *human energy crisis*. Every year there are hundreds of thousands of reported (and even more unreported) cases of child abuse. It is the cause of the highest rate of death of children under five years of age. Over half the victims of abuse are under two years of age. This reflects on the miseducation of the parents. And adding inestimably to the human energy crisis is faulty education in the grade school. Children who are victims of permissive upbringing, where discipline is lacking, often grow up to be uncooperative and disruptive, if not outright destructive. Little wonder that most of the crime in the United States is committed by adolescents between the ages of 13 and 21.

Knowledge of the whole human being—including body, soul, and spirit—should be basic to education, else we educate only half-men or quarter-men. To bring reality to life, our present age must deal with the soul and spirit as well as with the body. Then, even the body will assume new significance, for when it is understood to be the instrument of the spirit-being of man, the body will be seen as a sacred temple. So it was regarded before the concept of the indwelling spirit was abolished by church decree in the ninth century A.D. In the last centuries, materialistic science has gone on to present us with concepts of both nature and man which are devoid of spirit—a necessary phase of development to attain full ego consciousness in freedom. However, since the modern view of the universe as a machine and of the human being as an animal has undermined education, it has left in its train problem-filled generations resorting to "therapy" and an educational system terrorized by violence. Our machine culture has resulted in many persons becoming to a large degree heartless, soulless, and inhuman.

Of course, there are still countless insightful teachers and promising pupils who prove that their soul and spirit have not been blighted by the destructive frosts of cold intellectualism, materialization, mechanization, and animalization. Social healing will occur in proportion as wholeness is restored to our image of the human being and of his or her relation to and significance in our spirit-filled, living cosmos. If we really want to live in the present and prepare for the future in the right way, it is essential that consciousness be enlarged, for instance, to include the concept of repeated earthly lives.

The coming of a soul-spiritual being from supersensible spheres to incarnate in a body on earth is a long, difficult process whose magnitude we should seek to comprehend, and which we should gently assist; but in our age it has all too often become a rude awakening, and sometimes, unwittingly, a cruel one. No one would think of demanding that a musician give a concert on an instrument still in the process of construction. Yet it has become popular to start educating a child in infancy; although premature functioning causes strain and weakness, not strength, and cripples the child's future unfolding.

Each seven-year period unfolds a new stage of reorganization and growth. We have shown that in the first seven years, ruled by the reflecting Moon, the child learns by *imitation*. If the child's environment is imbued with moral strength, he or she will experience the world as *good*. During the second seven years, ruled by Mercury, the child learns through respected *authority*. If the wonders of the world and of man are presented pictorially and artistically, the child experiences the world as *beautiful*. Having these soul treasures the child can more easily meet the crisis of the third birth at puberty—that of the individual astral body that ushers in adolescence.

In the Moon cycle from birth to 7, growth forces proceeded primarily from the head, and in the Mercury cycle, 7–14, from the rhythmic system. In the Venus cycle, they extend further downward to the metabolic-limb-reproductive system. In the minds of most people this physiological change is the mark of puberty. It certainly is important, but not all-important, for there is also a change in psychological-consciousness. This may be confusing unless one realizes that the two streams move in opposite directions, the former moving downward, and the latter upward.

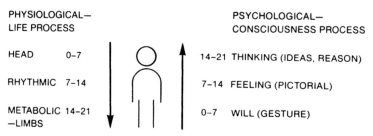

PHYSIOLOGICAL—
LIFE PROCESS

PSYCHOLOGICAL—
CONSCIOUSNESS PROCESS

HEAD	0–7		14–21	THINKING (IDEAS, REASON)
RHYTHMIC	7–14		7–14	FEELING (PICTORIAL)
METABOLIC	14–21		0–7	WILL (GESTURE)
—LIMBS				

The two streams of physiological and psychological growth

In the Moon cycle from birth to seven years, when the two streams are at opposite poles, they create no conflict because body, soul, and spirit still function as a unity. In the Mercury cycle after the second dentition, when soul forces are freer, they both work harmoniously in the rhythmic system, at least until the age of about 10 when there is the first astral quickening. But with the birth of the independent astral body at puberty and the emergence of the individualized spirit, the two streams are again at opposite poles, the physiological in the lower organism and the psychological in the head. This sets the stage on the one hand for *love*, and on the other for *new mental powers*. The independent intellect can now be active in reasoning, thinking logically, discriminating, and making judgments. Heretofore the organization was not mature enough for this kind of independent mental activity. To the previously gained assurance that the world is good (birth–7), and that it is beautiful (7–14), can now be added the idea that the world is *true* (14–21).

The body changes rapidly and not in equal proportions. There are awkward dangling arms and legs. That the body is not under full control is evidenced in a boy's voice. It is more disturbing than if you were to return to your home and find it rearranged and in the process of being altered. No wonder then that at this age the awkward adolescent experiences inward turmoil, uncertainty, fear, insecurity, bewilderment, and contrariness. The heightened sensitivity is apt to take things as hurts that were not intended to be so. Everything has to be newly validated, including the adolescent's identity within the totality of humanity and his or her own place in the world. The inner being, brought from the spiritual world and other earthly lives, now breaks in mysteriously and emerges more clearly.

The adolescent is both lovable and pitiable. Beneath the outer veneer of self-confidence, carelessness, irresponsibility, disinterest, impoliteness, even rudeness and insolence, there is a longing for comradeship and a need for heroic idealism. Elders now need to be understanding, have love, patience, and humor, and should give tactful support. If the adolescent has this support, and *if* his soul has not been ossified by materialism and premature intellectualism, there will, ideally, emerge a quest for the heart of the world. It is a quest for what transcends the beast, a quest for true heroes and heroism in the encounter with reality.

Rightly, the element of love has always been associated with Venus. At puberty, on entering the Venus cycle (14–21), a new power of love is born. Before puberty, while still enveloped in the astral sheath of the world—as the embryo was enveloped and nourished by the body of the mother before physical birth—the child has general feelings of sympathy and antipathy. With the birth of his own independent astral body he advances from generalized to individualized feelings.

Feelings now are extremely alive. Since the youth is now endowed with the capability of procreation, these feelings give a preoccupation with sex if they manifest only on a physical level. The trend of modern materialistic and intellectual education, of the media, and of psychiatry is to direct attention toward sex, to say the least. When nature is viewed materialistically and the human being as a higher animal, souls become empty and starved. Then, as L. Francis Edmunds aptly states, "Soul-starvation is interpreted as sex starvation,"[1] and love is equated only with sex.

On the other hand, love is ennobled when one beholds the world as the work of art of spiritual Beings, with the human body a temple for the spirit of man, and society one organism where each person fulfills a necessary function. The endeavor during the Venus cycle should be to develop love for knowledge—love for knowledge of the outer world, love for ideas, love for one another, love for all human beings, and love for humanity in its universality. It is tragic when an adolescent leaves school or loses interest in and enthusiasm for knowledge and for life, and reverts to brutal will and destructive deeds, thus making the temple into "a den of thieves." It is tragic when the good, the beautiful, and the true are, out of emptiness of soul, driven out, or degraded and destroyed by drugs or illusory "highs."

It is tragic, too, when education exalts the intellect above all else—witness I.Q. and scholastic aptitude tests—as though man were head without heart. Brotherliness and cooperation should be honored as well as intellectual achievement and a high I.Q. (fortunately becoming passé). Intellect alone, not balanced by feeling and will, does not lead to truly constructive action. Lifeless concepts are like barnacles, hampering the progress of life's proper unfoldment.

Although it sounds paradoxical, an inversion of qualities does occur as life unfolds. There will not be true *liberty* or freedom later in life unless there was worthy imitation during the first seven years. Adults will not practice *equality* if revered authority was not

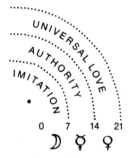

The quality of the Venus cycle
(14–21) added to those before

The Venus cycle

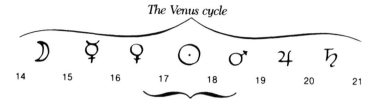

14   15   16   17   18   19   20   21

experienced from 7 to 14. And *universal love,* developed during the
Venus cycle of age 14 to 21, prepares one for *fraternity* in adult life.
Thus, by educating children rightly in the first three successive
seven-year periods of life, they can become adults in whom are
manifested the three goals of liberty (freedom in the cultural
sphere), equality (equal rights in government), and fraternity,
(brotherliness in economic life).

It is shown in both the Moon and Mercury cycles how the seven-
year period unfolds according to a planetary order, a sequence that
can no more be changed than can the paths of the Moon and Saturn
in the sky. The first three years are ruled by the three inner planets,
the Moon, Mercury, and Venus. The fourth is the central Sun year.
Then come the three outer planets, Mars, Jupiter, and Saturn. The
same law applies to the Venus cycle, 14 to 21. Only brief hints will
be suggested here. It is hoped that once one is familiar with the
pattern, one will be able to observe its application in each individual's unfolding. In this way one can work more consciously in
accord with cosmic laws.

The Moon, 14 to 15
The influence of the Moon in the first year of the Venus cycle
contributes to the rapid growth and bodily changes and to the functioning of the reproductive organs. It also moves in the seething
forces of feeling and the tides of the emotions. In the first year of
earthlife, the mirror quality of the Moon reflected all impressions
from the environment. At 7 years it reflected soul forces, and now at
14 it reflects the spirit, opening the way to individualized thinking.

Mercury, 15 to 16
Mercury, in the second year of the Venus period, makes thoughts
and feelings more articulate. The study of artistic speech, poetry,
and laws of meter is helpful. The learning process is promoted by
polarities and contrasts, e.g., in art, by black and white drawings;
and in chemistry, by the polarity between acid and alkali. In

ancient history, note that mankind descended from a more spiritual awareness to the conquest of physical life on earth, whereas now we should be rising out of materialism to a spiritual orientation. In history and literature contrasts can be shown between love based on blood ties (Arjuna, Edda, Hector) and individualized love (*Niebelungenlied,* Achilles, Romeo and Juliet). Acting in a play can be an important experience.

Venus, 16 to 17

This is the strongest Venus influence in all of life because it is the Venus year of the Venus cycle. After the worst turmoil of puberty and a better adjustment to the body, one becomes "sweet sixteen"! The sweetness turns sour if self-centeredness, vanity, and pride prevail. But the sweetness can become heavenly fragrance if the soul bears beautiful blossoms of gratitude, unselfish love, logical reasoning, thoughtful deeds, and perhaps even willingness to make sacrifices.

Venus bestows the beauty of love and a love of beauty. Color, music, and eurythmy, alongside study of the achievements and limitations of modern science, foster balanced, harmonious development. In the Steiner schools this is the year when the main theme is Parsifal. In literature and history, light is shed on the quest for the Holy Grail and on the maturing of the individual in the process of his or her striving toward the goal of ideal adulthood.

The Sun, near 17 to beyond 18

The Sun irradiates the central portion of every seven-year period. Its influence blends into the preceding Venus year and extends through the following years of the outer planets. The Sun strengthens the sense of self. An intensified consciousness of the uniqueness of each specialized self will not result in egotism if the self is always seen in relation to the whole. The last year of high school should include a survey of all the fields of knowledge previously studied, and present a comprehensive view in which the true picture of human beings and their place in the world stands out clearly. The *Curriculum for the First Waldorf School* states for the 12th class: "If his teachers have fulfilled their responsibility in educating him, he can go forth into the world morally strong and intellectually ripe, and with an open heart can find his own tasks." "Our highest endeavor," said Rudolf Steiner, "must be to create free human beings who, out of their own initiative, can impart purpose and direction to their lives."[2]

Mars, 18 to 19

With the increased sense of self conferred by the sun, adolescents will react more individually as the world opens to them in greater fullness. In addition, the soundness or the flaws in the unfoldment before 18 will be revealed. If he or she has developed clear thinking and a widened heart, the adolescent will be able to cope with the situations to be faced, either in further schooling or in practical life. From Mars will be derived the needed courage, energy, and enterprise. However, if the soul structure was not properly prepared, Mars can incite rebellion, making the activist, the noisy radical and, at worst, one who resorts to destruction and violence.

The First Nodal Cycle

During the Mars year everyone experiences the first nodal cycle. The plane of the ecliptic (the apparent path of the Sun through the zodiac, or real path of the earth around the Sun) and the plane of the Moon's orbit around the earth, do not coincide. They are at an angle of about 5°. The two points where the planes meet are known as the Moon's nodes. One is the ascending or north node, also called the dragon's head. The other is the descending or south node, or dragon's tail.

Because of the earth's nutation—a movement comparable to the wobble of a spinning top—the Moon's nodes slowly change position, receding about three minutes of space every day. After 18 years, 7 months, 11 days, they complete the circle of 360° and return to the place they occupied at one's birth.

In the months before and after their return to the natal place, they provide gateways to new awareness, for they attune the soul (Moon) to the spirit (Sun). Since the soul and spirit are outside the body in sleep and are then enriched by the worlds of soul and spirit, the nights during this period are very important. Usually one has significant dreams to which one should pay heed. Often this cycle marks a crisis in one's life, with outer as well as inner changes. Always it offers an opportunity for new orientation.

Jupiter, 19 to 20

Jupiter's benevolence combines well with the overall Venus influence in the year from 19 to 20. Whether it is helpfully expansive or unwisely extravagant, and whether its optimism is well-founded or unjustifiable depends on the wisdom one has brought from previous earthly lives, one's earlier training in this incarnation, and the new direction taken during the nodal cycle.

Saturn, 20 to 21

The last year of every seven-year cycle is ruled by Saturn. To the weak, this last year of the Venus cycle may bring discouragement and obstacles that seem insurmountable. There may be a tendency to withdraw and to be unsocial. To the strong, hindrances become stepping stones to greater achievement, and one becomes more patient, steadfast, serious, and responsible.

At 21 one reaches adulthood. Although the voting age has been lowered from 21 to 18, it takes three cycles of seven for the physiological stream to flow downward from the head to the feet, and for the psychological process to move upward from the feet to the head. Usually, the ego organization is not complete until the age of 21. With the completion of the Venus cycle, the individual is then ready for further unfolding in the first of the three seven-year Sun cycles.

7

THE THREE SEVEN-YEAR
SUN CYCLES, 21–42

THE BIRTH OF THE "I" AT 21 AND
THE SENTIENT SOUL CYCLE, 21–28

WHAT joy it is when a soul-spirit being, descending from worlds of spirit and soul, is welcomed lovingly and understandingly into the earthly realm! What joy it is—even though sometimes fraught with suffering—to witness its life's unfolding through infancy, child-hood, and adolescence, and then its entry into adulthood as a self-conscious, responsible, independent individual!

However, in the impatience of our Western civilization, in the hurry to get ahead, and in the loss of connection with the spiritual cosmos, cosmic-rhythmic laws are ignored. Nerves get on edge, tranquilizers are resorted to, addiction to damaging, dangerous drugs is epidemic. For many souls life becomes disordered, in-harmonious, empty, and devoid of meaning and purpose. How sad it is when a soul-spirit being, descending from luminous worlds of spirit and soul to enter a physical body, is immediately plunged into a stark, dark material world, and is prematurely rushed into adulthood!

With life's right unfolding, adulthood begins with the birth of the "I", or ego, at 21. The whole human being is present all the time, but only gradually can it manifest.

The preparation of the threefold body to become the instrument of the ego requires three births: the physical, the etheric (at the change of teeth), and the astral (at puberty). It also requires three cycles of seven years: the Moon cycle 0–7, the Mercury cycle 7–14, and the Venus cycle 14–21. At 21 the fourth birth occurs, the birth of the "I," or ego, when the Sun sphere of influence is reached.

We have seen that in each Sun subyear of the cycles of the inner planets there is a progressive awakening of ego activity. In outline, here are the observable effects of these Sun years: Moon cycle, Sun year, 3–4 (2⅓ to 4⅔), first utterance of "I," as yet only a mirror-like reflection of the true I. Mercury cycle, Sun year, 9⅓ to 11⅔, beginning of separation from the world. Venus cycle, Sun year, 16⅓ to 18⅔, sense of unique self, yet related to the whole. This is the "quickening" of ego awareness during the "embryonic" development of the ego organization which takes place during the Venus cycle, 14–21. Not until 21 is the ego organization complete. Those who have recently concerned themselves with adult life cycles have, with some justification, connected early adulthood with ages 17–40. But the "quickening" of the ego at 17 should be differentiated from the "birth" of the ego at 21. It should not be overlooked that 17–18 is a Sun subyear of the Venus cycle, whereas 21 begins the first Sun cycle.

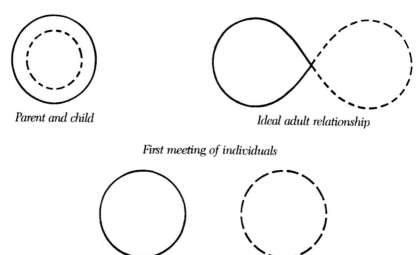

Parent and child   *Ideal adult relationship*

First meeting of individuals

Changing relationships

Pictorially, one might represent the changing relationship between parents and child as a metamorphosis from the concentric circles of diagram 1 to the lemniscate of diagram 2. It is hoped that at no stage in life will the two entirely separate circles of diagram 3 be applicable to the parent-child relationship. Physical birth places full responsibility on the parents (diagram 1). Gradually teachers and others share the responsibility until the ego becomes self-guiding at 21. Although all education should be oriented toward the goal of inner freedom, children are not capable of inner guidance. The goal is not reached if freedom is granted too soon, as is the case when permissiveness prevails. When permissiveness is allowed before the ego is capable of inner guidance, the youth may become little more than an animal moved by instinct, and sometimes even more dangerous. Every animal is a member of a species under the direction of a group-soul. Adolescents who rebel against and sever themselves from their parents tend to seek shelter in a kind of "group-soul" of their peers. Until they become adults they still need, on a decreasing scale, some sheltering influence from a person with ego maturity. From 21 onward, ideal adult relationships are indicated in the lemniscate (diagram 2). It portrays how persons, while maintaining their own individualities, keep a free flow of communication and exchange with each other.

Adults who meet for the first time are represented by the two separate circles of diagram 3, for adults meet as separate individualities. In order to establish a wholesome relationship there should be a metamorphosis from the separate circles (diagram 3) to the lemniscate (diagram 2). At no time should diagram 1 enter into the picture, not even a slight absorption of one circle by the other.

Relationships easily become strained when one person belittles another and does not respect the ego of the other. It may happen that one tries to impose his or her will on another, where one wants to remake others to conform to one's own standards, instead of accepting them as they are. The hardest lessons in this respect are apt to occur in the marriage relationship, where there were less problems in earlier times when male dominance was accepted, just as there are less today in lands where it is still recognized. At present in the Western world, individuality has attained a high development, recognizing the equality of men and women; hence the dominance of one person over another becomes an outrage against individuality. In milder forms of dominance, one ego tries to influence and coerce the other in subtle ways; in more severe instances, it becomes an absorption, a dictatorship that suppresses the free expression of the ego of the partner.

True marriage and genuine friendship are portrayed by the lemniscate (diagram 2) in which there is contact and exchange from each half of the figure to the other, yet each maintains complete wholeness. That is, each ego maintains its complete individuality. There is freedom, complementation, and enrichment for both, and both willingly make sacrifices for each other. Thereby they not only bless each other, but their union or association benefits everyone they contact, and it contributes to the advancement and harmony of the cosmos.

The story is told that a student of Rudolf Steiner once asked him how she might influence her husband to share her interests. He reproached her for wanting to exert such an influence. He said that she should not even in her thinking wish to change him. Any change must arise from within in freedom. The chief factor in adult relationships is respect for the ego of others.

The ego is the sharp two-edged sword of Revelation, the Apocalypse of St. John. On the one hand, the ego can be selfish, wholly self-centered, wishing to exalt itself, to possess what rightfully belongs to others, and to be at war against other egos. On the other hand, the ego is what makes man an individual self-conscious being, the crown of earthly creation. It gives the human being inner freedom and independence. The divine basis in man is the ego.

In the course of cosmic evolution, the ego is a relatively new member of the human being, hence it is sometimes said to be still a baby. The truth of this is evident when one compares its stage of development with the perfection of the physical body, our oldest member. The mission of the earth is to perfect the ego so that in complete freedom and independence it expresses love. When that goal is reached, the earth will be a planet of love, as now it is a planet of wisdom. Wisdom is inherent in everything. We find it in the structure of every blade of grass, every blossom, butterfly, bird, and bone, and in the integration of the whole of nature. If we carry forward the evolution of the earth as intended, then the entire earth will become an embodiment and manifestation of love.

In the course of the single human life's unfolding, the ego does not come forth "full-fledged" at 21, any more than did the physical body at birth, the etheric body at the second dentition, or the astral body at puberty. However, instead of seven years, the ego requires three times seven years, the period from 21 to 42, to attain its full potential in a given incarnation. This indicates the importance of the "I," which is one's very own possession, not inherited, not transmitted by father and mother. It is one's own essential being which one brings from repeated earthlives.

The three cycles of seven likewise indicate the importance of the Sun in our solar system and during life's unfolding. No single cycle of seven years, as applies to the inner and outer planets, befits the Sun. During the Sun cycles from 21 to 42, the ego gains experience and understanding of the world and of itself by working on the development of the threefold soul. The true ego or I is itself spiritual. It must, however, experience itself within the threefold soul: the sentient soul from 21 to 28; the intellectual soul from 28 to 35; and the consciousness or spiritual soul from 35 to 42. Thus gradually the temple lights up from within.

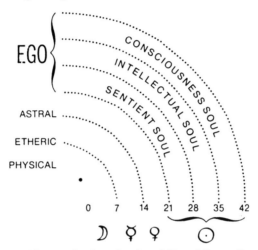

The ego develops the threefold soul (21–42)

During the first Sun cycle, 21 to 28, the ego works on the *sentient soul*. By means of the sentient soul, inward feelings arise in response to sense impressions. It embodies our reactions to the world. For example, when we enter a room, we become aware of the size and the color of the room, and aware of the people around us. The perceptions are provided by the sentient body (the astral body), whereas the conceptions, the inner images, are in the sentient soul, as also are our inner feelings in response to what we observed.

Sense perceptions have increased immeasurably in the last centuries. Think of the relatively few sensations people had several centuries ago: They did not travel much. They had few books, no radio, and no television. Perhaps what they lacked in variety of sensations was compensated by the depth of their feeling of intimacy with nature. Now we are flooded with sense impressions. We can select from countless programs, books, and associations. We can travel extensively with ease. Or, we can push a switch and have the world brought to us in our homes. Instead of etching scenes deeply into the memory, many people depend on the camera to replace memory.

Coming to us in superabundance, impressions are all too rapid, fleeting, and superficial. This superficiality and the restless desire for changing sensations undoubtedly are factors contributing to the high rate of divorce among young adults in their twenties, and among older adults who have not matured beyond the sentient soul.

Persons in the sentient-soul stage tend to live in the present moment, oblivious of the past and the future. They are motivated largely by the sensations connected with their feelings—their desires, likes and dislikes, sympathies and antipathies, pleasures and aversions, instincts, urges, and passions.

When the sentient soul responds to an event with anger, this might bode either good or ill. On the one hand, if it is an outburst of rage arising from egotism, it poisons the soul, weakens the ego, and isolates one from the world. On the other hand, when anger flares up as a reaction to injustice, it can be an educator of the sentient soul still untempered by the intellectual soul and the consciousness soul which develop later. Such "noble anger" indicates that one is not an indifferent spectator; it is a mark of independence, and of opposition to wrong in the outer world. As one matures and conquers anger, it is transformed into love. "A loving hand is seldom one which was not sometimes clenched at the sight of injustice or folly."[1]

Historically, the cultural age that specialized in developing the sentient soul was the Egypto-Chaldean-Babylonian-Assyrian. Today, the sentient soul predominates in the Italians and in all Latin peoples; in general they are more emotional. In the course of every person's life-unfolding, the sentient soul period, from 21 to 28, is the time for sentient experience and creative adventure.

The sentient-soul Sun cycle

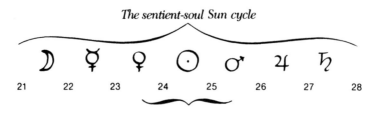

In describing the inner planetary cycles, generalizations were given for each successive year of each seven-year cycle. After the birth of the ego there are more individual variations of application. Nevertheless, the same planetary influences, in the same order, still hold. Keep clearly in mind that the first three years of each seven-year period are ruled respectively by the change-producing, nurturing Moon, the agile Mercury, and the lovely Venus. Then comes heightened awareness and increased activity of the ego in the fourth year, the central Sun year. In the sentient soul cycle the Sun year is between ages 24 and 25. The last three years are marked by the widening influence of the outer planets: the aggression or the energy and courage of Mars (25–26); the extravagance or the wisdom and expansiveness of Jupiter (26–27); and the depressing or the consolidating forces of Saturn (27–28).

If you are in this age group, 21–28, you can see how your life is unfolding year by year in harmony with this planetary pattern. If you are beyond this cycle, a retrospective survey might reveal new insight into the order of events.

The study of biographies can be made more fruitful by using this planetary key to life's unfolding. Biographies then become intensely interesting and awe-inspiring. For example, a few weeks after Tennyson's twenty-fourth birthday, his most beloved friend, Arthur Hallam, died. In the "Life and Work of Alfred Lord Tennyson," excerpted from the two-volume *Memoir,* his son stated that this death caused "a crushing grief" and an "overwhelming sorrow." "But such a great friendship and such a loss helped to reveal him to himself." In what year did this revelation of his self occur? It was in the Sun year of the sentient-soul Sun cycle.

THE INTELLECTUAL SOUL, 28–35

The second seven-year Sun cycle begins around the age of 28. During the first Sun cycle, 21–28, the "I" or ego was dimly brooding in the sentient soul while receiving sense impressions and experiencing a feeling response to them. In the second Sun cycle, 28–35, the I shines forth in the *intellectual soul,* thinking on what is perceived and becoming more conscious of itself. It knows *"I AM an I."*

As the name indicates, the intellectual soul—also called the rational or mind soul—is concerned with understanding, with knowledge, with finding the meaning of things. If you are under 28, you may believe that you already think much. But you will find when you reach the age of 28 that a change does take place. There is no physical manifestation as there was with the change of teeth at 7, or with puberty at 14. It is a subtle inner change within the soul, a shifting of emphasis from developing the sentient soul to unfolding the intellectual soul.

The intellectual soul seeks understanding in the light of thinking. It enables us to reflect on external impressions, to ponder over them, and to combine them in the mind, thus leading to greater independence from the influence of the outer world. Instead of taking in impressions rather passively, the intellectual soul actively thinks on them and also on sense-free ideas. Aspiring to truth, it produces concepts and ideas that are sharply defined and formulates clear judgments. It seeks to establish a balance between the outer and the inner. In the course of evolution, the intellectual soul developed during the Greco-Roman cultural age, giving rise to logical thinking and philosophy, and to a harmony between the outer and inner world. At present this soul predominates in the French.

Lacking an ego and the power of thinking, animals have no intellectual soul. The less developed a human being is, the less he exercises thought and reason. At first thought serves only the sentient soul, making possible the gratification of the desires and needs.[2] A person who employs thought selfishly to seek only his own ends becomes an egotist. In its higher expression, the activity of the ego in the intellectual soul strives to cultivate a sense of truth. In order that the ego may experience truth in the intellectual soul, the sentient soul must first be cleansed, else passions and desires may intervene and either cloud or distort the truth. When the intellectual soul permeates feeling with the inner light of thought, the ego purifies and refines the soul so that it masters and guides the feelings, thoughts, and volitions, giving clarity of thought and directing thought to sense-free understanding.

During the sentient soul cycle, young people are apt to live mostly in the present moment, the present sensation, for the present is most important for the sentient soul. When one comes to the intellectual soul stage, the thinker transcends the present; he spans time, connecting the past, the present, and the future.

The First Saturn Return
The new relationship to time, however, is the result not only of the change from the sentient soul development to the intellectual soul, but also to the *Saturn return* which everyone experiences sometime

between 28 and 30. Saturn has then completed its orbit and for the first time returns to the position it occupied at one's birth.

A few months after she moved to another borough, a friend called me up and told me what a tumultuous period she had been passing through. She found herself changing in many ways. She was trying to evaluate people. Instead of thinking superficially about their outer appearance, she was probing into their real being. For a time she had put her studies aside and now she was coming back to them. This description prompted me to ask, "How old are you?" She replied, "Twenty-eight. I'll be 29 next month." After I described the nature of the Saturn return, she said, "That fits me perfectly. Now I understand what is happening to me."

During the year when Saturn is approaching its natal place, it prompts one to: "Stop! Look! Listen! Take stock of yourself, face yourself in truth, not as you thought you might be, but as you really are. Change yourself and your attitude toward life." Above all, this is a most introspective and self-analyzing period, and results in seeing oneself in a new light. One reviews the past, reappraises it without sentiment, and makes a reassessment. One asks oneself, What have I really accomplished? Reevaluation leads to such questions as: What capacities do I have? What limitations? What are my opportunities? One revises one's way of life, establishes new goals, and sets new aims for oneself.[3]

The ego, the "I," must be in command. It must be strong in a selfless way, and assume responsibility, saying: "I am responsible for what has happened to me. I must blame myself, nobody else, for my life's destiny. I am responsible now for how I shape my future. I have grown up, I have put away childish things. I am mature." One young woman who all her life had been tied to her mother's apron strings, when she reached this age, wrote: "I'll have no more smothering." She could not free herself until she "came to herself" as an ego being at this age.

Thirty is a significant age. It is not by chance that people talk about being older after 30, because the Saturn return will have occurred by this time. One should have become a different human being, become twice-born. Most of the changes occur within one-self, but often there are changes in one's environment and in human relationships. Sometimes it breaks up marriages, at least those based solely on sentient soul experiences. When one partner grows into the intellectual soul and the other does not, he may begin to wonder, "Why did I choose, and how have I lived with, this person?" This may lead to a break, or at least a crack, in the relationship, unless the more mature soul understands and waits for the younger one to experience the Saturn return and respond to the unfolding intellectual soul influence. Of course, souls vary in this response. Some fail to meet positively the Saturn challenge. The less progressive continue to feel rather than to think.

The following three examples of the Saturn return will be designated X, X^{100}, X^n. Sometimes it is helpful to speak out of experience. The lone X represents my experience. When I was 24½, I went abroad to teach in an American school in Bulgaria. This travel during the sentient soul period brought multitudinous new impressions into my life. When I was nearly 28, I met someone who belonged to an esoteric Brotherhood. For the first time I heard about man's connection with the cosmos and ideas about reincarnation. Half a year later, I met a large group of the Brotherhood, including the Initiate Teacher. At that time I knew nothing about the stars, and it was not until years later that I checked the time of my Saturn return. I could identify the time precisely because the climax occurred on New Year's Eve, two months before my thirtieth birthday. That very night, Saturn was exactly on my natal Saturn!

In the preceding months I had been agonizingly examining my life. During vacations one of us had to stay at the school, and it was my turn to be on duty. Alone that Christmastime, the self-examination intensified. On the last day of the year I determined that I would not go to sleep until the stock-taking was resolved. Like Jacob wrestling with the Angel, I felt, "I will not let go until you bless me." It was not until 4 o'clock New Year's morning that I really did feel the blessing. After only a couple of hours of sleep, I arose early, for I had promised the minister and his wife to accompany them in visiting some of the townspeople that day. I was far more alert than if I had had many hours of sleep. I was vitally alive, for my life had taken on a new dimension. I knew in what direction I would go. The resolve was made. I look back upon that experience with gratitude, knowing that I had come to grips with myself and my destiny, and I had set my feet firmly on a path toward a definite goal.

The second example, X^{100}, is that of Rudolf Steiner. In his autobiography, he stated: "When I look back upon my life, the first three decades appear to me as a chapter complete in itself. At the close of this period I removed to Weimar to work for almost seven years at the Goethe and Schiller Institute. The time that I spent in Vienna between the first journey to Germany . . . and my later settling down in the city of Goethe I look upon as the period which brought to a certain conclusion within me that toward which the mind had been striving. This conclusion found expression in the preparation for my book, *The Philosophy of Freedom*." Steiner had to find a world-conception which included his own being, for if one cannot find the being in oneself, how can one find being in the world? Therefore he was concerned primarily with a mode of thinking.

Thinking plays a crucial role in finding oneself, for it is the self who thinks, not the brain, which is the instrument of the thinker. "Thinking has the same significance in relation to the idea as the eye has to the light."[4] We have an organ of sight which gives us perception of light. We have ears to give us perception of sound. And we have a thinking faculty to give us perception of ideas. It is just as clearly a sense organ as are our other senses. Steiner wrote, "My world of ideas was moving in this direction when the first chapter of my life ended with my thirtieth year."[5] "At the close of this first stage of my life it became a question of inner necessity for me to attain a clearly defined position in relation to certain tendencies of the human mind."[6] Our age will only gradually catch up with what Rudolf Steiner achieved at the time of his first Saturn return.

The third example, X^n, puts us on holy ground. By means of spiritual vision in the Akashic Record or Memory of Nature, Rudolf Steiner described the so-called hidden years before Jesus of Nazareth was baptized in the Jordan by John the Baptist.[7] The Gospel of St. Luke, 3:23, plainly states that the baptism occurred when "Jesus himself began to be about thirty years of age." Preceding the baptism and coinciding with the Saturn return, Jesus looked back over his experiences since his twelfth year. He told his mother how he had felt excruciating pain at having found, between the ages of 12 and 18, that in spite of the depth and wonder of the Hebrew heritage, it no longer had the power to meet the needs of that day.

Between the ages 18 and 24, outside his home environment, in places where the heathen Mysteries had prevailed, he found that they had deteriorated to such an extent that demons instead of higher beings were invoked at the ritual. The realization that they had nothing to offer hungry souls caused him tremendous sorrow.

His third experience, from 24 onward, concerned the Essenes. They had attained a high degree of spirituality, but at the expense of others, for they isolated themselves and they did not meet the needs of the masses. In the agonizing experience of looking back and feeling the utmost compassion for the hungry souls who were as sheep without a shepherd, the ego of Jesus made way for the Christ Ego to enter his physical, etheric, and astral bodies at the baptism, an event that brought a turning point in all Earth-evolution. This is the X^n, that is, raised to the nth degree, to infinity.

In studying biographies, it is revealing to observe the effect and importance of the transition from the sentient to the intellectual soul and of the Saturn return. For example, Gautama Buddha was 29 when he received his enlightenment. My own experience at the Saturn time changed the direction of my life. The experience of Rudolf Steiner changed the direction of thinking in our century, although humanity for the most part is not yet aware of what was achieved. This period in the life of Jesus of Nazareth had the most far-reaching significance not only for himself. The descent of the Christ at the baptism affects not only all mankind, but the entire evolution of the Earth and of the cosmos.

The Incarnation of the Word

Profound awe and reverence are evoked when one contemplates the magnitude and sublimity of the Christ Event and its correspondence with cosmic laws. As the Sun is the center and heart of our solar system, so the Christ, the highest, most sublime Being of the Sun, is the central leading Cosmic Spirit. He is the primal and primary creative Being, the Cosmic I, the Logos-Word, guiding world evolution, including human evolution. In the course of ages he approached ever nearer to the earth until the time was ripe for his Incarnation. That ripeness occurred when Humanity was emerging from group-consciousness—"I and Father Abraham are one"—and maturing to the stage of self-consciousness, ready to experience "I am an I."

As in the individual the I AM experience unfolds in the intellectual soul, so in the development of humanity as a whole it occurred in the cultural age specializing in the development of the intellectual soul, namely, the Greco-Roman age, 747 B.C. to 1413 A.D. Just after the first third of that age had passed, "The Word became flesh and dwelt among us (and we beheld his glory, the glory as of the only begotten of the Father), full of grace and truth. . . the law was given by Moses, but grace and truth came by Jesus Christ" (St. John1:14,17).

"The Word became flesh" when Jesus of Nazareth sacrificed his physical, etheric, and astral sheaths to the Cosmic Christ Ego at the baptism by John in the Jordan. As Christ Jesus he walked on the earth during the three years from 30 to 33.[8] Not only do these years correspond with the central Sun section of the second Sun cycle, but when one surveys all three Sun cycles as a whole, one sees that it is central in the three.

	☽	☿	♀	☉	♂	♃	♄
Sentient Soul	21	22	23	24 · 25	26	27	28
Intellectual Soul	28	29	30	—31 · 32—	33	34	35
Consciousness Soul	35	36	37	38 · 39	40	41	42

The three Sun cycles

The baptism at 30 falls in the Venus year into which the Sun year radiates. During the first forty days in solitude or loneliness (usually translated wilderness), Christ Jesus overcame the temptations of pride and arrogance, of both fear and reckless courage, and of enslavement to the material world. Only gradually could the Christ identify with the earthly body of Jesus of Nazareth; only gradually could the God become man. Much of the first year was devoted to a more silent ministry, before Christ Jesus, during the Sun year proper, undertook active teaching and more public ministry. With the beginning and advance of the Mars year, 32–33, opposition increased, culminating in the crucifixion, April 3, 33 A.D.[9] With infinite love he bore infinite suffering, the prototype of the greatest ego strength and mastery and, at the same time, the greatest selflessness.

The death on Golgotha took place on the earth, yet it was a supersensible event. With the flowing of the blood, the Christ-Sun forces suffused the aura of the earth with an astral light which will eventually become etheric light and finally physical light. The most atrocious death thus became the seed for a new sun in the universe. The worst of the Mars year was succeeded by the vast expansiveness of Jupiter. Saul, who became Paul, did not see Christ Jesus in the flesh, and he could not believe that the crucified one could have been the Christ, until on the way to Damascus he clairvoyantly beheld him as the solar Being in the aura of the earth. Then he knew with utmost certainty that he who had suffered the ignominious death on the cross was indeed the Risen One, and that he had vanquished death and united himself with the earth.

As a living Presence in the earth, the Christ works as the renewing, life-giving, and soul-and-body transforming power now and throughout all the future evolution of mankind. The death on Golgotha became the insurance of new life and implanted the seed of eternal egohood, a goal of earth evolution. The Resurrection is the guarantee of the continuance of the evolution of the earth and man through all cycles of time to come. (Saturn rules time.)

Ever since that Central Event during the intellectual soul development of mankind in the Greco-Roman age, there is in the intellectual soul stage as the single human life unfolds, the possibility for the individual human being to experience "I am an I" and to enrich the I. "Through the Christ Impulse the human soul became conscious for the first time that an Ego, an 'I,' was to find a place within it, a self-conscious 'I' through which in the future course of Earth-evolution there must be revealed all the secrets formerly revealed by the astral body through natural clairvoyance."[10]

Since the Christ Event, the temple of the soul lights up within when the I shines forth, fully conscious of itself as an individual ego, free from heredity, and drawing its noblest qualities from the sublime Sun Being, the central figure of earth evolution, who says, "I AM the Light of the World." "I AM the way and the truth."

Light and Truth

It is common practice to link "light" and "truth." Truth is inwardly experienced as light. When a truth is grasped, we say, "I see." One can observe how the eyes and face light up when understanding dawns. When we strive for truth, the hallmark of the intellectual soul, we expand beyond ourselves. The light of truth frees us from our self-centered selves and we unite with the world, whereas untruth, lies, falsehood, and lack of a sense of truth estrange and alienate human beings. With these negative qualities we associate darkness.

In striving for truth in the intellectual soul, the ego takes its own education in hand. In the inner planetary years, especially the first two—Moon 28–29, and Mercury 29–30—while the Saturn return is experienced, thinking is directed primarily to the past. The Sun year 31–32 (more accurately, 30⅓ to 32⅔) is most opportune for the ego to shine forth within. In the years ruled by the outer planets— Mars 32–33, Jupiter 33–34, and Saturn 34–35—there can be greater inner freedom to contemplate the future with composure, inner tranquillity, and clarity. One is then approaching the great divide at 35, and life's continued unfolding in the consciousness soul.

THE CONSCIOUSNESS OR SPIRITUAL SOUL, 35–42

As beings of soul and spirit, each of us on entering earthlife is endowed with a rich heritage of spiritual forces, enough to sustain us to the age of 35. By 35 this spiritual capital is used up. It sustains us during all the nurturing, upbuilding, and preparatory cycles of the inner planets, and through the first two Sun cycles, by which time we achieve our egohood in freedom and become fully responsible for our further development. Thirty-five is the great divide: It divides the world that was given to us from the new world to which we must give birth. We ourselves determine whether or not after 35 we acquire the spiritual capital needed for our future maturing to take an ascending path, and for us to create out of the spirit. *Freedom* and *responsibility* of the highly individualized ego are hallmarks of the consciousness soul.

The ego that was still only dimly brooding in the sentient soul, and that attained greater clarity and shone forth in the intellectual soul, develops its fullest clarity and an even higher, richer life in the consciousness soul. Not until the consciousness soul cycle is entered can there manifest the "pure, unalloyed ego" coming into its own in freedom. No longer is it passively swept along by the tides of pleasure or pain and the emotions of the sentient soul, nor is it content to brighten and maintain its inner light as it did in the intellectual soul cycle. To be man in the fullest sense of the consciousness soul, the ego must continually enrich itself, be creative, and radiate from its Sun center what will, in turn, enrich the world. This can be achieved if one progressed beyond self-awareness and beyond self-knowledge of "I am an I," to clear self-consciousness of the spiritual nature of the I, and to the discovery that within the Sun temple of the soul is a Holy of Holies.

Thinking directed beyond the personal to that which is eternally true and truly good, kindles an imperishable light in the Holy of Holies. However, the initial stages of the consciousness soul development bind the soul strongly to the body, with the result that one becomes much more ego conscious as an independent being who looks out into the outer world, objectively observes external reality, and works within that world. By thus sinking into the body and encountering the external world, one achieves individual freedom, and ever-increasing ego capacity and creativity.

Through the activity of the consciousness soul one disentangles oneself from personal likes and dislikes, espouses truth apart from sympathy, and genuine goodness apart from personal advantage or disadvantage. Educators of the consciousness soul are: a sound sense of the ego, full self-possession, love and devotion (not weak submissiveness, but the ego active in the will), response to duty, and willing self-sacrifice. Instead of relying on outer directives, one follows one's own intuitions which derive from spiritual sources. For the pure, unalloyed ego emerges as "the kernel of human consciousness" which in reality is rooted in the divine.[11]

The pattern of unfolding in the single earthlife reflects what occurred in mankind's evolving. In far, far distant prehistoric epochs, before the earth became solid, the germinal beginnings of the three soul forces were added, one by one, as the form of man-in-the-making metamorphosed as the Earth condensed from fire, to air, to water; that is, from one unified cosmic entity to the separation of the Sun, and later the separation of the Moon. In those early stages our souls were in the sheltering care of spiritual Beings. These Beings guided us as our development gradually proceeded. We have indeed come a long, long way to our present independent egohood.

The task of the Egypto-Chaldean civilization, from 2907 to 747 B.C., still under divine guidance, was to develop the sentient soul; and that of the Greco-Roman, 747 B.C. to 1413 A.D., the intellectual soul. In 1413 our modern age began and will continue until about 3573, so we are just over a fourth of the way through the age of the consciousness soul. In the intellectual soul age, man still felt himself a member of the universe, whereas in our age he has become conscious of his *freedom* and his own power of resolve and action. The English and Americans have the consciousness soul most naturally; others have to strive to attain it. Freedom and equal rights were basic principles in the founding of the United States of America, which celebrated its Bicentennial in 1976.

Through countless aeons higher Beings worked selflessly to bring us where we are today. The realization of this truth calls forth in our souls a sense of infinite *gratitude*. And the awareness of the truth that whatever is to be achieved in the future depends on our creativity, and our voluntarily reaching up to higher Beings, calls forth a sense of infinite *responsibility*. Increasingly we see how unproductive and destructive is the opposite view: "The world owes me a living." "I have it coming to me."

If the consciousness soul is to function constructively in our era, it is essential that we acknowledge our vast debt to the divine powers of the cosmos for their sacrifices from "In the beginning." It is also essential that we assume individual responsibility for the present and the future, contributing to world evolution through our own effort, and working to our utmost capacity. Having become ego conscious beings, we must take our development consciously in hand. This requires strength of *will* and devotion.

In the course of an individual's maturing as life unfolds, the sentient soul period relates to feeling, the intellectual soul to thinking, and the consciousness soul to *will*. The activity of the ego in the threefold soul thus consecutively correlates with the members of the threefold body, but in reverse order of development. Also, the quality of character in each soul reflects the nature of the upbringing in each of the corresponding bodily members. For example, if plasticity is preserved in the physical body and the imitative child is surrounded by love and happiness from 0 to 7, the character in the consciousness soul period, 35 to 42, will be open and relate freely to the world, whereas unkindness and pain, 0 to 7, result in a closed character from 35 to 42.

"I" in

↑ 14–21 astral body	—feeling	—sentient soul	21–28
7–14 etheric body	—thinking	—intellectual soul	28–35
0–7 physical body	—willing	—consciousness soul	35–42 ↓

The threefold soul in the threefold body

To begin with, the consciousness soul brings us deeply into the physical body. This promotes strength of will, which enables us to take vigorous, effective hold of life. The physical body is our instrument for carrying out the deeds prompted by the ego working in the consciousness soul; it makes it possible for us to be active in the

physical world. The very form of the human physical body with its
upright posture (portrayed by the Egyptians in the obelisk), the
head lifted toward the Sun, and the free use of the hands, is designed to be the bearer of the ego. Conscious of this from the spiritual point of view, one realizes more than ever the tremendous
significance of the physical body and physical world at the present
stage of the earth.

In the process of diving down completely into the body and
severing ties with the spiritual world, man has attained freedom
and enhanced his ego consciousness. This enables him to view the
external world objectively as an observer or spectator, and to master
the material world. At the same time, this engenders doubt or even
denial of the spirit. To understand the working of the consciousness
soul in the individual, one needs to know the nature of the consciousness soul age in which we live, for individual destiny inter-
twines with the destiny of mankind as a whole in any given era.
Most persons have not yet advanced beyond the initial materialism
of our age. In 1917 Rudolf Steiner said that materialism would
continue to increase for four or five more centuries.

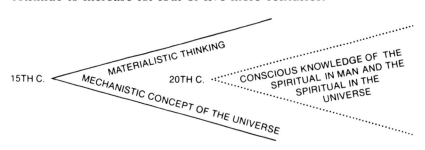

The historical development from materialism to spiritual consciousness

However, there are signs of change in our twentieth century. At
the beginning of this century, Steiner presented a spiritual world-
conception in a fully conscious manner, derived, not in trance or in
mediumism, or in unclear, illogical sentient soul mysticism, but in
a heightened, fully ego conscious manner. "We are only preparing
for the preparers, as yet nothing more,"[12] he said. At present the
number of vanguard souls is increasing rapidly, and soon there will
be millions and millions. Nevertheless, for modern souls, steeped
in the materialism of our time through their upbringing and education, changing streams requires a reversal of will-impulses in order

to overcome the deep-seated, ingrained habits, and conventional ways of looking at life. It should not be overlooked that in changing streams there lurks the danger of wanting to escape from earthly duties.

"The goal of spiritual science is to guide the whole man into the higher worlds, not merely the thinking man but also the man of feeling and of will. . . . *Spiritual knowledge must be received into the will.* When we absorb spiritual knowledge in its true meaning, something works within our soul like a spiritual Sun."[13] It is the spiritual Sun that gives *insight* into the true nature of all things and is not deceived by outer appearances. It penetrates to the super-sensible within the sense-perceptible, to the spirit in matter; hence it is "more radiant than the Sun." This *insight* guards against alienation from the world and gives new meaning to our earthly tasks.

With more than a fourth of the cultural age of the consciousness soul behind us—the period that gave rise to doubt, fear, and apathy—we are approaching the central *SUN* manifestation of this era. Therefore we can henceforth call this third soul not only the consciousness soul but the spiritual soul, as Steiner later suggested. In the unfolding of the individual life, one may still experience doubt during the early years of this third Sun cycle when the inner planets, Moon, Mercury, and Venus, are sub-factors. But with the Sun influence extending before and after the middle year of the seven, one may become capable of grasping the spiritual nature of the ego.

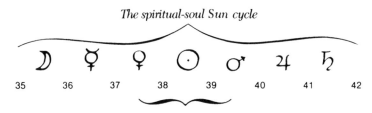

The spiritual-soul Sun cycle

During the sentient soul cycle, the Sun temple of the soul has only a dim light within, while the outer world with its sense-impressions is still of primary interest. In the intellectual soul cycle, the temple lights up within as the "I" shines forth fully aware of itself and knowing "I am an I." In the third Sun cycle, especially in the middle Sun portion, the spiritual soul opens the door to man's Holy of Holies, the innermost and most sacred part of the

Sun temple of the soul. One then knows that the true essence of the ego is divine. As a drop is to the ocean, so the I is to God. It is not God, but is of like nature to God. Some souls at this stage experience consciously the Sun Being, the Christ. As Mary Fullerson was told, "You need not search for the Holy in a distant quest. You need only realize its Presence at the altar of your dedication to My Atonement, My Overcoming, and My Life within."[14] A helpful meditation is this stanza:

> More radiant than the Sun
> Purer than snow
> Finer than ether
> Is the Self
> The Spirit in my heart.
> I am this Self
> This Self am I.[15]

Once one has experienced this essential being, this true self, one has an identity of one's own, and is secure in oneself, not dependent on acceptance or rejection by others. But having found this self, one is duty bound to this very self not to seclude oneself. Illuminated and enriched with the inner Sun radiance, one must go forth into the outer world. To the unenlightened it may seem to be a trivial or a hard world, whereas the enlightened one sees it in its spiritual character, and freely pours forth upon it the riches of his radiant self. Thereby he enriches the world, makes the spirit operative in the outer world, and creatively contributes to the process of world-becoming.

The Second Nodal Cycle

Very significant is the fact that during this third Sun cycle everyone experiences the second nodal cycle at twice-18 years, 7 months, 11 days, that is, around the time one is 37 years, 2 months, 22 days, although its influences are usually felt months before and after. The meeting of the Moon and Sun forces at the nodal point provides a gateway which opens the soul world to the spirit world, bringing in new streams of forces and new awareness. One manifestation is in significant dreams. Coming as it does in the dawning of the Sun section of the third Sun cycle, this second nodal return can, if one is ripe for it, relate one to the Christ in some exceptional way.

Rudolf Steiner's second nodal cycle occurred in 1898. In his auto-biography he describes the intense spiritual testing he experienced from 1897 to 1900, from age 36 to 39. "I learned to know fundamentally where lie the forces of the time, striving away from the spirit, disintegrating and destructive of culture, and from this knowledge came a great access of the force that I later needed in order to work out of the spirit."[16] He knew that the spirit must be found *in* the world of man and of nature, not relegated to an impenetrable world "beyond," as traditional Christianity and philosophers such as Kant maintained. This brought him into conflict with the demonic Ahrimanic powers which promote a purely mechanistic-materialistic way of thinking so that knowledge of nature does not lead on to knowledge of the spirit underlying nature.

"The true substance of Christianity began germinally to unfold within me as an inner phenomenon of knowledge. About the turn of the century, the germ unfolded more and more," wrote Steiner. "Before this turn of the century came the testing of soul I have described. The unfolding of my soul rested upon the fact that I had stood in spirit before the Mystery of Golgotha in most inward, most earnest solemnity of knowledge."[17]

A few years ago, at the time of his second nodal cycle, a young man who had previously not been able to relate to spiritual science began to assimilate it avidly, and one night was astonished when a fantastic light penetrated his being and he became conscious that his true inner being was like a spiritual Sun. Jewish by birth, the Christ had had no meaning for him, but now he understood the relationship of light, the Sun, and the Christ. As a result of this experience, which became totally ingrained in his nature and developed new capacities in him, he has an ever-continuing source of strength to sustain him in the redirecting of his will and its application in pioneer endeavors to make the spirit operative in daily life.

A corollary to grasping the spiritual nature of one's own I is the recognition of the spiritual nature of the ego in *every* human being, regardless of distinctions based on class, nationality, sex, color, heredity, or religion. Each person is a distinct individual on his or her own merit. In the modern individual, developing the consciousness or spiritual soul, there is a purely human element that can relate to what is purely human in others, untouched by appearances. Only on this basis can true community be realized. There will be no danger of it being a herd of weak "moral zeros" dominated by authoritative power, which is community without individuals. Nor will it be a group of self-seeking, isolated individuals without community. It will be a community *of individuals.*

Another corollary is that we respect the freedom of others, even as we want them to respect our freedom. Much of modern business, especially advertising, relies on influencing people. A criterion for evaluating both business practice and religious movements is the degree of freedom they grant to the individual and in turn expect from the individual. The goal of the evolved spiritual soul is *ethical individualism,*[18] in which each person, out of the very core of his or her free being, decides what is right for that unique self in each given situation as conditions change.

Human beings manifest the entire gamut of soul development. At one extreme is the hardened materialist with muddied sentient soul, whose passions interfere with the activity of the ego in the intellectual soul through undisciplined, unreasoning distortion of the truth. Such a person has an inflated ego that seeks to grasp everything for itself without regard for other egos, not even respecting their right to live. Yet in his inmost soul such a person is lonely, afraid, and empty, and easily sinks into despair. In the course of repeated earthlives, with their interim destiny-appraisals by spiritual Beings in the spiritual world, life-experience serves, at first unconsciously, to transform, refine, and expand the threefold soul.

Advanced individuals, out of the forces of their spiritual soul, work on their own transformation, consciously fashioning the three souls to bring forth their unique potential. When permeated by the forces of the spiritual soul, the sentient soul is purified and exalted; then it glows with fervor, adds warmth and enthusiasm to all one's undertakings, and becomes the embodiment of *beauty.* The Mars year, 39–40, is especially suited for this, though development in all three souls may occur simultaneously.

During the next year, 40–41, with the help of Jupiter, one may widen and enlarge one's knowledge of the world, gain far-sighted wisdom, and make the intellectual soul a clear focus for *truth.* Before 35, the intellectual soul sharpens the intellect and we acquire knowledge. After 35, the spiritual soul, especially in the Jupiter year, provides the opportunity for a higher manifestation, namely, wisdom. Tennyson viewed the relationship between knowledge and wisdom thus:

Who loves not knowledge? . . .
. . . Let her work prevail.
But . . .
Half-grown as yet, a child, and vain—
. . . .
A higher hand must make her mild,
    If all be not in vain; and guide
    Her footsteps, moving side by side
With Wisdom, like the younger child:

For she is earthly of the mind,
    But Wisdom heavenly of the soul.[19]

Toward the end of his Jupiter year, Tennyson's "In Memoriam," on which he had worked for seventeen years, was published, bringing glory and fame. And his long-awaited marriage brought joy and peace. Five months later, following soon after his forty-first birthday, the Saturn year bestowed on him the well-merited honor of becoming the poet laureate.

In the Saturn year, 41–42, one stands erect on the high pinnacle of the spiritual soul period, yet with feet firmly on the earth, and heart attuned to the Sun-heart of the universe and to all human hearts. With firm resolve, will, and readiness to make sacrifices, one responsibly imbues matter with spirit. Then the evolved forces of the spiritual soul itself will manifest genuine *goodness*, as expressed in this stanza:

    The soul's creative might
    Is striving from the heart's foundation
    To kindle to their rightful working
    The powers divine in human nature,
    And it itself to fashion
    In human loving and in human action.[20]

THREE LEGENDS RELATING TO THE THREEFOLD SOUL

In their search for meaning in life, many young people today are turning to folklore, sagas, myths, and legends. There are three legends that correlate with the three soul principles—the sentient, intellectual, and consciousness souls. They present profound truths for modern man in pictures that may be more telling than words alone.[21]

King Arthur and the Round Table

In the evolution of mankind, the sentient soul developed during the Egypto-Chaldean civilization. In an individual life's unfolding, it is most active during the first seven-year Sun cycle from 21 to 28. The legend which reflects the sentient soul in modern form for the highly individualized Western person is that of King Arthur and his Round Table. When the Egyptians and Chaldeans looked up to the stars, they saw spiritual beings. The Sun, the Moon, and the zodiac were to them living spiritual realities. In the legend of King Arthur, the cosmos is humanized! The Sun is represented by King Arthur, the Moon by Queen Guinevere; the twelve signs of the zodiac by the twelve knights of the Round Table.

The knightly deeds of slaying monsters and rescuing the defenseless portray the ego's activity in the sentient soul to refine and purify the astral body. One illustration of the sentient soul approach, out of the many in Tennyson's *Idylls of the King,* is Gareth, the youth whose mother, typical of some mothers who have children come of age, opposed his leaving home to go to King Arthur's court. Gareth pleads:

> . . . In me put force
> To weary her ears with one continuous prayer,
> Until she let me fly discaged to sweep
> In ever-highering eagle circles up
> To the great Sun of Glory, and thence swoop
> Down upon all things base, and dash them dead,
> A knight of Arthur, working out his will,
> To cleanse the world.[22]

The sentient soul has enthusiasm, and often impatience. It has the potential to reform or to deform—to cleanse what is base in itself and in the world, or to destroy, either senselessly or using even violent means to satisfy its selfish desires. Like man, animals have a sentient soul, but they have no ego; therefore they immediately obey their instincts. Much of modern culture cultivates the concept that man is an animal. Little wonder then that he acts like an animal, following his instincts, impulses, and passions uncontrolled by that in him which distinguishes him from and transcends the animal, that is, the ego, the Sun power, the King Arthur in him.

It is helpful to keep in mind that from 21 to 28 the sentient soul is still not yet as curbed by intellectual soul reason as it will be after 28, or by the sense of individual responsibility conferred by the consciousness soul after 35. In this seven-year period of the sentient soul, the first three years, 21–24, ruled by the inner planets— the Moon, Mercury, and Venus respectively—are the most vulnerable to instinctual behavior. The ego should be strengthened by the Sun year, 24–25; gain in courage in the Mars year, 25–26; in wisdom during the Jupiter year, 26–27, and in serious purpose during the Saturn year, 27–28.

The Holy Grail

The secrets of the intellectual soul in our modern age are revealed in legends of the Holy Grail. As an individual life unfolds, the ego shines forth in the development of the intellectual soul in the seven years from 28 to 35, the central one of the three Sun cycles. For mankind as a whole, the intellectual soul evolved during the Greco-Roman civilization, the central one of the seven post-Atlantean civilizations, the one in which the sublime Sun Being, the Christ, incarnated on earth, thus making it possible for the I-Am-an-I consciousness to shine forth in every individual human soul.

In the early centuries of Greek culture, there still was a final echo of the ancient Mystery wisdom, whereas our present-day intellect is directed almost exclusively to the material world, devoid of spirit. The transition from the spiritual wisdom of the past to the spiritual aridity of our modern intellectuality took place gradually, until the beginning of our modern age in the fifteenth century. Since then the transition has been increasingly rapid.

In this process a change occurred in man's physical organism as well as in his soul. Although the physical change can be seen only by a spiritual seer, not by physiologists, the effects are evident in the soul. At the time of the Egyptian culture, the universe was still experienced as alive. Now it is regarded as lifeless, and man no longer receives life-giving, up-building spiritual impressions with his perceptions. Meanwhile, certain threadlike currents in the physical and etheric body have become lifeless, and what was once vivid in the soul has become unconscious. These lifeless elements in the body, and the unconscious ones in the soul, are subject to withdrawal from the rule of the soul, from ego control. This has produced a split.

The lifeless portion, withdrawn from the rule of the soul, is open to the attacks of invisible beings that lead man astray. The Luciferic forces engender sensuality, pride, egotism; they lure one into illusory states through drugs and alcohol, and alienate one from earthly responsibilities. The Ahrimanic powers, on the other hand, sink man so deeply into the material world that he believes that spirit does not exist, and that the clever intellect and material gains are the only goals.

The split has resulted in a double nature. Even so great a soul as Goethe experienced and aptly described this duality: "Two souls, alas, reside within my breast,"[23] one espouses lust, and the other wants to sever itself from the dust and aspire to heaven. In earlier times, such disharmony was not possible. In modern times, because of the lifeless elements in our organism, the intellectual soul is more open to attack than it was in the Greco-Roman age, or still is in the East. It is the intellectual soul that divides into the two sides manifesting as a double nature, referred to as Dr. Jekyll and Mr. Hyde since 1886, when Stevenson wrote his classic by that name. Another commonly used expression now is "split personality." This split accounts for the statement, "I don't know why I did it."

In picture language we can speak of this duality as the Castle of the Holy Grail and the Castle Merveil, that is Montsalvat and the domain of Klingsor. The Holy Grail is the new wisdom of the spirit, which can so enrich and strengthen the living portion of the soul that it can be lord of what has become lifeless and unconscious. This situation is still little known in the East; hence Eastern wisdom is not suited to meet the soul needs of modern Western mankind. Klingsor is the enemy of the Grail who practiced black arts, and who compelled Kundry to seduce Amfortas, the Grail King. Amfortas thus became wounded in body and soul, was deprived of the Holy Lance, and experienced untold suffering. The Klingsor forces have intensified in our twentieth century, using blatant, rampant sexual aberrations, black magic, and every form of materialism in education, technology, science, and the news media, to deaden what remains living and to make the intellectual soul completely barren, parched, and empty. A college teacher, proud of her intellectual attainments, attended an anthroposophical class for a time and very capably explained any passage assigned to her. After some months she said that Anthroposophy was the most ingenious, fabricated world conception imaginable. The sacred substance of the Holy Grail had no reality for her.

Parsifal

Since the fifteenth century we have been in the age of the development of the consciousness soul, which unfolds in the individual from age 35 to 42. The secrets of this third soul principle are revealed in all that concerns Parsifal. Briefly, the consciousness soul makes great demands on the individual, who in freedom must now be on his own. He should be conscious not only of himself as an I, as in the intellectual soul cycle, but of the spiritual nature of the I, and should assume full individual responsibility.

Parsifal, or Percival, means "through the vale," through the valley of trials, the path of every modern soul. On his first visit to the Castle of the Holy Grail, Parsifal did not understand what he saw, and he was too immature to ask questions. Cast out of the castle and into the outer world, he had to overcome apathy and doubt, and pass through tests before he could reach "Saelde," blessedness. When tempted by Kundry, Parsifal, "the timorous fool," was victorious through the compassion he felt for Amfortas's suffering. Finally, "through search and suffering," his will reinforcing his inextinguishable search for spiritual understanding, he returned *consciously,* on a Good Friday, to the stronghold of the Holy Grail.

What Parsifal achieved was not knowledge based on any authority but on conscious experience of the Holy Grail. He vividly realized how the earth itself became the chalice to receive the purified blood of the Savior, which gave resurgence of life and new meaning to all existence. This spiritual mystery he made his own in his consciousness soul. Then he could redeem Kundry and heal the wounded Amfortas, thus restoring to a unity the divided nature of the intellectual soul.

In order to comprehend the world and oneself spiritually, one must descend into the body completely and become conscious of one's freedom, before cognizing the spirit in the body and in the world of matter. Thereby the consciousness soul becomes the spiritual soul. Then one can become a law unto oneself without infringing on the rights of anyone else, for "All men's good be each man's rule."

Each individual is a Parsifal, especially after the age of 35. Each one should be asking questions, should overcome seductive temptations, become possessor of the Holy Lance, heal the wounded Amfortas, and redeem Kundry. Each one should become king in one's own inner Temple of the Holy Grail, not abandoning the world but working healingly in it with full self-consciousness, devotion, and self-sacrifice. Then, like Parsifal, one becomes "the help-bringing knowing one."

8

THE MARS CYCLE, 42–49—
THE DANGEROUS FORTIES OR
DYNAMIC COURAGE

ALTHOUGH life's unfolding is described as taking place in seven-year periods, each having a distinctive character, we should never lose sight of the fact that life is one whole. From conception to death it is a unity, as is the body a unity. Think how vastly different in appearance and function are the head and the feet! Yet the body is a unified organism in space. Similarly, *a human earthlife is a unified organism in time*, despite the difference between the infant and the aged person.

Damage is done, resulting in problem-filled personalities, when children are expected to mature too soon and are deprived of childhood; also, when the elderly will not acknowledge their years. Using another comparison, one does not make the mistake of expecting fruit from a tiny seedling, nor prevent a grown tree from bearing fruit. Figuratively, however, this is the all-too-common practice in human life. It is a strange paradox that children are expected to forego childhood and be too grown-up, whereas the elderly want to forego old age and remain young.

"Seldom nowadays do we find people with gray hair and wrinkles welcoming with joy the dawn of each new year because each year brings new possibilities of development to the organism; and new knowledge unattainable before is within reach. We should actually retain the possibility, all through life, of rejoicing in the coming year, because each year charms forth the divine-spiritual content of our own inner being in ever new forms. I want to emphasize this point. We should really and truly learn to experience our life as capable of development not only in youth, but through its whole span between birth and death."[1]

One of the marvels of our universe is its infinite variety. Looking around us on the earth, and looking up to the heavens, we are awed at the unending diversification, and yet the harmony of the whole.

Within our solar system the differentiated, moving planets maintain an order which, as has been pointed out previously, is reflected in our life's unfolding, following a pattern of seven-year cycles, each of which is again divided into seven. We have seen that the inner planets, Moon, Mercury, and Venus are active from birth to 21. The influence of the Sun so far surpasses all the others that it extends throughout the next three seven-year periods, from 21 to 42.

Not yet described are the three outer planetary cycles, Mars, Jupiter, and Saturn, encountered respectively from 42 to 49, 49 to 56, and 56 to 63. The three groupings of three times seven—0 to 21, 21 to 42, and 42 to 63—correlate with the three aspects of man: body, soul, and spirit. From 0 to 21 the threefold body is prepared: the physical body, the etheric body, and the astral body. From 21 to 42 the "I" works on the threefold soul: the sentient soul, the intellectual soul, and the consciousness or spiritual soul. From 42 onward, the spirit can blossom in the as-yet germinal threefold spirit nature of man: the spirit-self, the life-spirit, and the spirit-man.

Members of man		Planetary life-cycles		Developed in
PHYSICAL BODY		0–7	☽	ATLANTIS
LIFE (ETHER) BODY		7–14	☿	ANCIENT INDIA
ASTRAL BODY		14–21	♀	ANCIENT PERSIA
EGO	SENTIENT SOUL	21–28		ANCIENT EGYPT-CHALDEA
	INTELLECTUAL SOUL	28–35	☉	GRECO-ROMAN CIVILIZATION
	SPIRITUAL SOUL	35–42		PRESENT: ANGLO-SAXON-TEUTONIC
TRANSFORMED ASTRAL	SPIRIT-SELF	42–49	♂	
TRANSFORMED LIFE BODY	LIFE-SPIRIT	49–56	♃	FUTURE AGES
TRANSFORMED PHYSICAL BODY	SPIRIT-MAN	56–63	♄	

The whole human being—
in individual earthlife and in the evolution of humanity as a whole

The diagram shows, in skeletal outline, the whole human being: the threefold body, the threefold soul, and the threefold spirit. It indicates when they unfold in the individual earthlife and also in the evolution of humanity as a whole. Not until future ages will the spirit nature of mankind develop, since in our present age the spiritual soul is still developing. Nevertheless, without this germinal spirit nature, no matter how exalted a person represents himself, he is only a dwarf, not the true stature as the human being he is meant to be. The spirit-self is the part of the astral body which the ego has already worked upon and transmuted from within the soul.[2]

If, from 0–21, the forces of life have flourished and not been deadened by our materialistic, intellectual culture, and if, from 21–42, the powers of the soul have developed in the sun radiance of a strong, Christ-filled ego, then from 42 onward, the aims of the spirit can flower and bear fruit. The fruit is a firm purpose in life that manifests in noble achievements which benefit all mankind. That is the ideal, an ideal attained by relatively few in our century, which has been barren of spirit.

If one comes to what Browning calls "The last of life, for which the first was made,"[3] and finds that the first was faulty, then the last of life may manifest flaws which were earlier not apparent; for, one was then still borne by the spiritual forces which brought one from the spiritual world through conception to about the age of 35. In the middle of life the growing and upbuilding process in the organism starts to be outbalanced by the destructive, declining tendency. The body begins to put up greater resistance, and the soul becomes weaker if it has not been nourished in freedom by a spiritually strengthened "I." Until this phase of life is reached, the materialistic, intellectual training may often seem effective and sufficient. Many may show signs of promise in youth. But unless the intellectuality is infused with spirituality, it cannot sustain one through the whole of the earthly life.

As a spiritual diagnostician aware of the acute illness of our civilization, Rudolf Steiner recognized the deficiency and prescribed the needed remedy: ". . . one would fain impress upon all true educators and teachers the urgent necessity of imbuing intellectuality with such spiritual strength that when the human being is passing through the later years of life, what has been permeated with moral force in his intellect may be able to hold the balance against the forces which draw him away" from the spirit.[4]

The intellectual training given in most schools and absorbed from the media and from the home, appeals only to the head (the brain and nerve-sense system), that is, to only one-third of the whole human being. The result of this one-sided development is that in "the middle man," (heart and lungs, the rhythmic system, the feeling aspect) there develops selfish egoism; and in the lower organism (metabolic-limb system, where will operates) passions and instincts hold sway. Persons thus afflicted become slaves of their instincts. Individually and en masse they make social claims and demands, but are themselves devoid of social feeling. This is the acute illness, the deadly disease, which our materialistic civilization has bred.

Over half a century ago in 1921, when the symptoms were outwardly far less obvious, Rudolf Steiner gave this prophetic warning: "If we allow things to take their course in the manner in which they have taken their course under the influence of the world-conception which has arisen in the nineteenth century . . . , we shall face the war of all against all at the end of the twentieth century. No matter what beautiful speeches may be made, no matter how much science may progress, we would inevitably have to face the war of all against all. We would see the gradual development of a type of humanity devoid of every kind of social instinct, but which would talk all the more of social questions. The evolution of humanity needs a conscious spiritual impulse in order to live."[5]

Life's unfolding after 42, during the cycles of the outer planets, Mars, Jupiter, and Saturn, will promote the evolution of the individual and of humanity if, during the spiritual soul Sun cycle, 35–42, one grasped the spiritual nature of one's ego. It is essential to know that what came before 42 largely determines what follows 42, when life unfolds in a more individual manner and when habits have become more fixed and are harder to change.

Mars is the first planet beyond the Sun, and relates to the first seven years after 42, that is, 42 to 49.

> The solar cycle comes to end
> As life upon its way doth wend;
> Mars' seven-year cycle then begins
> And promises dynamic things.

Mars is indeed dynamic. Mars is an agitator, inciting to intense activity and energetic action, whether it be constructive or destructive activity. A survey of the range of possibilities may be helpful for understanding the influence of Mars in one's own life and in the lives of others.

Again it should be emphasized that what happens in the Mars cycle depends largely on what preceded it. If the ego became infected with what has been described as the disease of our civilization, then this period will be what is often called, "the dangerous 40s." In that case, one lives to gratify the animalized desire-nature, and is apt to be combative, warlike, foolhardy, rash, impulsive, uncontrolled, and passionate. Anatomically, Mars rules the gall bladder. There is no mere chance relationship between gall stones and being galled (vexed, irritated). Mars is active, too, when, in slang usage, one has gall (effrontery).

If in the Sun cycles the ego rightly took command of itself, then in the Mars cycle one is in some measure courageous, master of self, enterprising, independent, self-reliant, and daring; one takes initiative, has strength of will and "iron" moral strength, espouses causes, and fights evil. Ardent resolution may manifest not only in outer action, but also in persuasive self-expression, for to Mars we owe our impulse to speech and the power of the word.

Iron, the metal ruled by Mars, can tell us something about the nature of Mars. Iron, and all that is developed out of it, has been indispensable in the construction of tools, buildings, bridges, means of transportation, and all the varied features of our materialistic civilization. Where strength is needed, Mars (iron) comes to our service. Mars (iron) also speaks to us of strength and courage when we behold the flaming sword of iron in pictures of Michael overcoming the Dragon.[6] Blake expressed the hope that the sword would never "sleep" in our hands until we have built (the New) Jerusalem.

Higher Beings in the cosmos are well aware of our need for iron in quite a literal sense. Every August and September they send to the earth showers of meteoric iron. When nature dies in the autumn, man's strength must not wane; it needs to be increased.[7] The presence of iron in the hemoglobin of the blood enables the ego freely to take initiative, and to be more resolute, assertive, and forceful. It is common knowledge that insufficient iron in the blood, causing anemia, hampers the ability of the ego rightly to perform its functions and weakens its power to be decisive, to make resolves, and to carry out resolutions.[8]

By using iron as a symbol, Tennyson accurately portrayed the transforming task of Mars, a task that is uppermost during the dynamic and dangerous forties.

. . . Life is not as idle ore,

But iron dug from central gloom
    And heated hot with burning fears,
    And dipt in baths of hissing tears,
And batter'd with the shocks of doom

To shape and use. Arise and fly
    The reeling Faun, the sensual feast;
    Move upward, working out the beast,
And let the ape and tiger die.[9]

Tennyson has Sir Galahad testify to the source of his strength:

My tough lance thrusteth sure,
My strength is as the strength of ten,
    Because my heart is pure.[10]

In the course of repeated earthly lives, through the aid of the courageous and dynamic Mars forces from 42 to 49, the enlightened ego will more and more "move upward, working out the beast," thereby transforming the astral body into the spirit-self. For the spirit-self becomes manifest in proportion as the I rules over the impulses and desires, and purifies and refines them; also, in proportion as thoughts are fructified by intuition in touch with spiritual realities; and in proportion as the will is strengthened and motivated by what is morally good.

Mars fosters independence and self-reliance. After 42, one is on one's own. Each individual should in freedom direct his own course and fulfill his own unique destiny. Hence specific directives for each year are not necessary. Once one understands the pattern of the successive planetary influences in the seven subyears of each cycle, one gains new insight into how the years unfold in accord with basic cosmic principles. We can experience it ourselves, and we can see it also in biographies. To illustrate this, the seven subyears of the Mars cycle will be correlated with typical events in the life of Rudolf Steiner when he was age 42 to 49.[11]

The Mars cycle correlated with the life of Rudolf Steiner

☽   ☿   ♀   ☉   ♂   ♃   ♄

42	43	44	45	46	47	48	49
February							
1903	'04	'05	'06	'07	'08	'09	'10

The development of Anthroposophy occurred in three seven-year phases. The first was within the Theosophical Society and was devoted to the spreading of spiritual cognition. Although dated 1902–1909, it broadly coincided with Steiner's Mars cycle, February 1903–1910. The founding of the German section of the Theosophical Society, with Rudolf Steiner as its General Secretary, occurred October 18, 1902, and he reached 42 on February 27, 1903. From the outset he made clear his independent position and manifested his courage in forging a path to the new, to a science of the spirit, and placing the Christ in the center of his teaching. "History without Christology is no true science." Very briefly, here are a few, out of many activities highlighting the planetary correlations.

1903, *the Moon year:* Change, move to a new location, initial growth of the movement; public lectures, with tours to many cities.

1904, *the Mercury year:* Wrote and published two basic books: *Theosophy: An Introduction to the Supersensible Knowledge of the World and the Destination of Man;* and *Knowledge of the Higher Worlds and its Attainment* (need for purification and inner transformation). Rhythms of Festivals. Student interest; lectures at universities, appealing to reasoned thinking.

1905, *Venus:* Lectures on art, music, social problems, speech (a holy, divine gift). Striving for improvement and cooperation.

1906, *the Sun:* Unflinchingly pursued the path of freedom of activity amid contradictory trends. In Paris presented a Christian (not Oriental) Theosophy to various nationalities. Two criteria for public lectures: "adapt to the consciousness soul" and "be scientific." Lectures on medicine, healing and education.

1907, *MARS:* "The year 1907 was filled with intense activity."[12] So Steiner's secretary, Guenther Wachsmuth, begins the chapter on this *Mars year of the Mars cycle.* Decisive in presenting "the inner force of the word." Delegates from many countries attended the Congress in Munich in May. Disagreement with Mrs. Besant apparent. Desired to maintain harmony (conflict is a waste of time), yet might possibly be compelled to take a stand.

1908, *Jupiter:* Expansion. "Ever-growing ramifications of . . . activities in every sphere of life. . ." Publishing burst former narrow confines; founded a private publishing office. Lecture tours in seven European countries; subjects comprehensive of the wisdom of the universe, but principally Christian esotericism. Twelve lectures on *The Gospel of St. John.* Boldly faced new tasks.

1909, Saturn: Concentrated on contrasting the past wisdom of the Orient with Western Esoteric Christianity. Lectures on "The East in the Light of the West." All of the East is in the West plus the light of the Christ. Rudolf Steiner and Mrs. Besant never met again after the Budapest Congress. Completion of *Occult Science—An Outline,* after 30 years of maturing (a Saturn return) making cosmic evolution accessible to modern thinking.

9

THE JUPITER CYCLE, 49–56—
EXPANSIVE OUTREACH AND UPREACH

As life proceeds its way to wend
When seven years of Mars are at an end,
The Jupiter cycle then begins
And offers more expansive things.

The expansiveness of Jupiter—the largest in size of the planets of our solar system—may manifest both as outreach and upreach. To each individual in modern times this means something different, ranging between two extremes. On the one hand, the materialist's outreach is to farther, faster movement and more possessions, and his or her upreach is toward personal power and pleasure. On the other hand, an evolved soul's outreach is to others, with compassion and self-sacrifice, and the upreach or aspiration is toward mature cosmic wisdom and great goals for all humanity.

We ourselves determine where we stand between these extremes. Background factors are: our record from previous earthlives; our relation to Jupiter in the period between our last death and rebirth; the nature of the Jupiter influence when we entered earthlife for this incarnation; our early training from birth to 21 in the three cycles of the destiny-determining inner planets, the Moon, Mercury, and Venus; our ego strength developed during the three seven-year Sun cycles, 21–42; and our self-control and courage in the dynamic Mars cycle, 42–49, the first of the three liberating outer planetary cycles. Jupiter then comes next, 49–56.

In general, Jupiter is the most liberating planet, providing broader horizons with new vistas, and an elevation of outlook that gives more objective views, puts everything in better perspective, and promotes tolerance. After the intensity of the preceding Mars cycle, the Jupiter cycle comes as a welcome mellowing and widening influence that helps to free us from our prejudices and prevailing mind-set, and increases our sympathy and open-mindedness. The transition from Mars to Jupiter might be compared to moving from the tension of a busy city to the calmness of a beautiful countryside where the air is clear and revitalizing.

One who responds positively to Jupiter is respectful, gracious, benevolent, generous, free, tolerant, merciful, forgiving, sincere, and primarily interested in quality. The negative response gives priority to quantity and appearance. It is never vicious or cruel, but tends to go to excess, lacking moderation; therefore it is extravagant, prodigal, wasteful, indiscreet; not candid, but hypocritical, self-righteous, and boastful. When the positive qualities stimulate willed action, there is an outreach to philanthropic endeavors; one gives dedicated service, bringing uplift to individuals, churches, charitable organizations, and institutions such as hospitals and prisons.

Jupiter can satisfy our yearning for wisdom. Our reasoning mind with its coordinating faculty we owe to Mercury, but wisdom-filled thinking and creative cosmic thoughts are the gift of Jupiter, "the Thinker in our planetary system."[1] Jupiter enables us to have a wide, elevated vision which in a living way portrays the cosmic present. All the present thoughts of the whole universe are in the keeping of Jupiter. Yet, because man is allowed to think as a free being, we must exercise clear, active, light-filled thinking of our own if Jupiter's revelations are to be brought to consciousness and not remain in the unconscious. It is encouraging to know that if we make sufficient sincere effort, the Jupiter Beings help us in sleep, making it possible for us in waking life to have an intuitive grasp of solutions to problems.

Through Jupiter we can have wise, fervent enthusiasm, our thinking can be mobile and vigorous, we can exercise sound judgment, and we can be blessed with common sense. This common sense and wisdom should become apparent in our speech. Whereas Mars often talks without thinking, Jupiter is more apt to think before speaking. Mars zealously tries to persuade; Jupiter calmly aims to convince, to satisfy the understanding.

The Jupiter cycle of life is characterized by what Wordsworth in his ode on the "Intimations of Immortality" called, "Years that bring the philosophic mind." Although the radiance and splendor of youth are gone,

> We will grieve not, rather find
> Strength in what remains behind; . . .
> In the soothing thoughts that spring
> Out of human suffering;
> In the faith that looks through death,
> In years that bring the philosophic mind.[2]

When Jupiter enlarges our understanding and matures wisdom, we shed rebellion and worry. We become philosophical, more resigned, harmonious, calm, serene, contented, joyful, hopeful, expectant, confident, optimistic, secure in the conviction that truly "all things work together for good to them that love God."[3]

This sense of security has decreased in proportion as materialism has increased. The more individuals have become proud of their achievements and looked upon themselves as the highest animal rather than as "a little lower than the angels,"[4] the more they lost confidence in a wise, ruling Providence. The more mechanized and lifeless their world became, the less they experienced the beneficence of Jupiter, even unconsciously. More and more people today perceive themselves as caught up in the materialistic bind of the cold, dehumanized, computer system.

The archetypes of the life forces in all the various orders of beings exist in the form of thoughts within Jupiter, "the Thinker in our planetary system." The prerequisite for renewed upreach to Jupiter is reverence, wonder, veneration, devotion. Only thus will thoughts again be filled with a life element and become attuned to the *livingness* in all the world—in human beings, in the earth, in the kingdoms of nature, and in the stars. In his writings and his humanitarian work, in word and deed, Albert Schweitzer was an outstanding example of reverence for all life.

Beyond, yet penetrating the physical world, is the astral or soul world, which correlates with the inner planetary spheres, the Moon, Mercury, Venus. Next is the heavenly or spiritual world, the Sun sphere, relating to the ego. "Beyond" this, in turn, is the higher spiritual world, whose subdivisions are the spheres of the outer planets. The Mars sphere is influential in transforming the astral body into spirit-self. Then comes *the world of providence,* the lofty spiritual realm of Jupiter, where exalted spiritual Beings, the great teachers of mankind, receive illumination from their cosmic inspirer, the Christ, who is to them as a Sun.[5] This is the plane of the life-spirit which bears a similar relation to the still germinal spirit nature of man, as does the etheric or life body to the bodily nature of man (see diagram on page 87). The life body is limited in size, whereas the life-spirit is capable of unlimited growth.[6] This growth occurs by transforming the etheric body into life-spirit, a longer and more difficult task than transforming the desires of the astral body into spirit-self, for it involves changing one's temperament, deep-seated habits, and character traits, such as forgetfulness, nervousness, tardiness, and indecision.

It will take many earthlives, in cooperation with the Christ-impulse, to achieve this transmutation until one's life-spirit in some small measure partakes of the exceedingly exalted nature of the life-spirit of the Christ, but earnest, conscious effort should be made. How is this accomplished? The best aids are art and religion. True art harmonizes and uplifts. Religion, in its outreach, forgives, maintaining an undisturbed harmonious relationship with others. In its upreach, it uplifts through prayer, meditation, reverence for the divine, repeated ritual, devotion to truth, and comprehension of the Christ Mystery.

It is not surprising, therefore, that during the Jupiter cycle of his life, February 1910 to February 1917, Rudolf Steiner gave first place to art, and to elaborating the anthroposophical understanding of Christianity. By means of his artistic creations—the Mystery Dramas, the new art of eurythmy, the building of the Goetheanum—science, art, and religion were brought again into a unity, as they had been in the ancient Mysteries, but on a higher level adapted to the present. It is revealing, even briefly, to highlight the planetary subdivisions of these expansive Jupiter years.[7]

The Jupiter cycle in the life of Rudolf Steiner

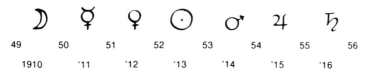

49	50	51	52	53	54	55	56
1910	'11	'12	'13	'14	'15	'16	

1910, the Moon year: First Mystery Drama, "The Portal of Initiation," led to idea of erecting a building as a home for the Society. 200 lectures had far-reaching effects. Among the lecture cycles were: "The Mission of the Folk Souls," "Genesis," "The Gospel of St. Matthew," which begins with hereditary descent. Announced the coming appearance of Christ in the etheric world.

1911, the Mercury year: Second Mystery Drama, "The Soul's Probation," attended by 800 from many countries. Polarities in lecture cycles, e.g., "From Jesus to Christ," "The World of the Senses and the World of Spirit," "Earthly and Cosmic Man."

1912, Venus: Lectures in eight countries of Europe; a unifying spirit. Third Mystery Drama, "The Guardian of the Threshold." Birth of eurythmy, the beautiful new art of movement. Birth of the Anthroposophical Society, "a feeling of joy passed through all of us." "The Gospel of St. Mark." Dornach, Switzerland, selected as the site of the building.

1913, the Sun: A new epoch in Christology: "The Fifth Gospel"; "Christ in the Twentieth Century"; "Christ and the Spiritual World." Emphasis on spiritual strengthening of the individual ego for the benefit of the totality; freedom, no "ought nots." Nine trips abroad. First public eurythmy performance. Fourth Mystery Drama, "The Soul's Awakening." Laid foundation stone for the building.

1914, Mars: Great activity in constructing "The House of Speech," a "living word" to bring souls into harmony; helpers from seventeen countries and all professions. Outbreak of World War I. Lectures relieved tension and had a tremendous inner strengthening and upholding influence. "Art in the Light of Mystery Wisdom."

1915, Jupiter year of the Jupiter cycle: Despite war conditions, tireless travel, giving encouragement, inspiration, hope-filled confidence, yet stressing the need for clarity of mind and truthfulness. The war an "inevitable consequence of thinking and action false to its very roots," e.g., relating man to the animal kingdom, not understanding the human being. First performance of the Christmas Plays, a work of art.

1916, Saturn: First half of the year, lecture tours; second half limited to and near Dornach, but reaching a wide public with knowledge right for the times, yet based on cosmic and human history. Such knowledge, inspired by art, opened the way to social action in the next seven years, the Saturn cycle. The Christmas plays were presented to war prisoners and the wounded—a social action at the very time when Steiner's third nodal return was exact. In November, "Karma of Vocation," lectures noting the importance of the nodal rhythm in the life of Goethe and for each individual.

The Third Nodal Cycle

The first nodal cycle, at 18 years, 7 months, 11 days, in the inner planetary cycle of Venus, relates more to the Spirit-God. The second, at 37 years, 2 to 3 months, in the last Sun cycle, relates to the Christ, the Son-God. The third, at 55 years, 10 months, at the end of the Saturn year of the Jupiter cycle, at the threshold of the Saturn cycle (56–63), relates to the Father-God, the will aspect. At this age the noted scientist, Swedenborg, had significant dreams (as happens at every nodal cycle) leading him "to relinquish his worldly ambitions and pride of intellect, and to submit his will completely to the Divine will"; then spiritual vision opened to him.[8]

10

THE SATURN CYCLE, 56–63—
AWESOME FATHER TIME

As life proceeds its way to wend
The Jupiter cycle comes to end;
The Saturn cycle now begins
And proffers one profounder things.

THE awesome figure of Father Time arises when we think of
Saturn. On leaving the expansive years of the Jupiter cycle, 49–56,
we enter the sphere of Saturn and should be prepared to face the
fact that the next seven years, 56–63, will be relatively contractive
and serious, requiring patience and a steadfast, firm will. The tute-
lage of Father Time will be productive of greater maturity, and
provocative of deep and profound thought. Wordsworth, after many
stanzas recalling the glory of childhood and later philosophic years,
ends his "ODE: Intimations of Immortality," with two lines that
describe the profundity of Saturn:

To me the meanest flower that blows can give
Thoughts that do often lie too deep for tears.

Father Time is often pictured holding an hourglass. No matter
how carefree one's life had been previously, the Saturn cycle calls
attention to the inevitable fact that we live within the bounds of
time as well as space, and that "time is running out." In some souls
this arouses fear, insecurity, and a melancholy mood. For others it
is a spur to more earnest, persevering, well-organized, dutiful
activity.

Father Time is also sometimes portrayed with a scythe, indica-
tive of his role as reaper. In this sense, we are made aware that we
must confront our destiny, reaping as we have sown in this life and
in previous earthlives. In the Saturn cycle the imperfections and
shortcomings manifest themselves and produce their fruit. To some
persons the reaper brings experience with death and the ensuing

100

loneliness or responsibility. If death does not strike close to home, one hears increasingly of friends and acquaintances being taken by the reaper.

In our mechanistic age we have a primary concept of time made visual by the clock, which measures all hours exactly alike. Yet life experience proves that, qualitatively, hours differ tremendously, as do days, years, and even minutes. In sorrow they seem to drag by with leaden feet and are loathe to leave, whereas in joy they speed away all too quickly. Saturn, Father Time, makes us more aware of the value of time and the accounting we give of our use of time. But above all else, Saturn is concerned with the past and the memory of the past. Each person has his own individual memory and can recall what occurred since the early years of his life. Similarly, Saturn is the faithful bearer and preserver of cosmic memory. It is the recorder of the entire history of all that ever happened in our planetary system, for it is in the initial and outermost planet having rise in our solar system. Uranus, Neptune, and Pluto have a different origin. So devoted is Saturn to the past that its influence upon us poses the danger of making the past too dear to us, of disliking progress, of wanting to bring back the past. Saturn insists on frequent retrospection.

The Second Saturn Return

Retrospection and scrutinizing introspection will be most active during the second Saturn return which occurs in the middle of the Saturn cycle, around the age 58 to 60. If one has rightly met the challenges of the first Saturn return, 28–30, this second one may not be so stressful, although there may be some sort of crisis and added responsibility. In some instances it involves employment and/or health, either one's own or the health of others. It signals that it is time to slow down one's pace and husband one's energies.

This double Saturn influence of the second Saturn return occurring in the Saturn cycle, can best be met by utilizing the support of the Sun forces, since the return comes in the Sun subyear. This Sun subyear promotes self-confidence and self-reliance in coping with changes and responsibilities, in making decisive resolutions, and in laying firm foundations for the rest of the life.

The Excarnating Process

Now let us take a retrospective look at life's unfolding from birth to the Saturn cycle. The element of disintegration sets in at birth, but the forces of life are so abundant that it is scarcely noticeable. Gradually, as life unfolds, the balance changes. Upbuilding forces decrease as the "capital" we brought from the spiritual world becomes exhausted around the thirty-fifth year, the midpoint of life. After 35, the mineralizing processes and physical decline increase, though the spiritual capital can be renewed by consciously relating to the spirituality of the cosmos.

We can also view this twofold process in a threefold way. The potentialities which the astral body brings from the spiritual world at birth work powerfully upon the body from birth to 21, developing the body as its instrument and completing the incarnation process. In the beginning years the animal nature predominates. At 21 the "I" with its self-consciousness is attained. From 21 to 42, using the body as its instrument, the "I" works on the sentient, intellectual, and spiritual souls respectively and enriches them by its experiences. From 42 onward, and increasingly in older years, the mineral nature predominates, the body puts up greater resistance, becomes less plastic, is harder, set in its ways, brittle, and sclerotic, thus "excarnation" gradually takes place.

As it has become fashionable to disregard the importance of how slow and gradual the incarnating process is, so there has been a deliberate blinding to how long and gradual the excarnating process is. It takes decades to incarnate. Likewise, it takes decades to excarnate. During the excarnating process, the astral body draws upon the etheric body, feeds on it, decreasing its vitality, its life-giving force. As life unfolds further, the etheric body draws more and more in turn upon the physical body, which thereby degenerates as one grows older.[1] The contrast between children and the elderly is vividly seen in watching them cross a street. Children fairly bounce across, whereas the aged cautiously step off the curb and shuffle across.

If in youth there has been merely materialistically inclined intellectuality without spiritual strength and moral force, then the spiritual stream dries up and in later life one may not be able to hold the balance against the destructive forces in the human organism. "Life in our time is often fraught with this tragedy and there is so much that does not stand the test of the years. In youth, ideals are plentiful; in old age few remain. Older people rely more upon the State and their pensions than upon the sustaining power of life itself; they need support from outside" because they cannot find the spirit within themselves and in the universe.[2]

Why is the Saturn cycle the vulnerable time for the onslaught of the destructive forces unless one is spiritually fortified? This we can comprehend if we understand the nature of Saturn and of its metal, lead. Lead is the heaviest of the seven metals related to the seven planets. Weight may be a disaster or a blessing, depending on the circumstances. If weight is added to an overloaded ship, it might submerge and destroy the vessel, whereas on another ship, lightly loaded, it could provide needed ballast and stability. Similarly, the heavy burdens of destiny that come during the Saturn cycle might cast one person into the depths of despair, gloom, melancholy, even physical illness, whereas to another it would serve as a challenge and opportunity to develop greater patience, persistence, steadfastness, strength of will, and practical ingenuity. The word "leaden" means heavy, hard to move, sluggish, dull, spiritless, or gloomy if applied to a mood or to thoughts. Saturn has this leaden influence on some souls, yet on others, weighty problems stimulate the greatest spirit-inwardness, will, and maturity.

What is the nature of lead? "Dense and sluggish, soft and pliable, yet of poor maleability and therefore easily broken when rolled or stretched; melted by a mere candle flame; of a quick fading lustre— this is lead, a chief representative of the baser heavy metals. The ways of the earth grip and affect this metal with ease; it can hardly defend itself."[3] Saturn and lead are very responsive to warmth. "Lead expands vigorously when heated and contracts strongly when cooled . . . Each particle of lead sucks in the heat, but only hesitatingly passes it on to the next."[4] What it gets, it retains and is slow to relinquish.

In considering lead and the human organism, the key factor is warmth. Initially, on Ancient Saturn—the first of three previous manifestations of our Earth in her long, cosmic evolution—man consisted of only a differentiated warmth organization, the basis of the physical body, which has meanwhile undergone many stages and transformations. Keep in mind that in the human organism at present there are two polarities of warmth: blood and bone. The ego is most closely related to warmth and expresses itself in polar opposites: in dynamics, and in form.

As dynamics, the ego works in the warmth of the blood through a dissolving process in which lead is most expansive. As form, the ego works in the bone system, the skeleton, through a hardening process wherein lead contracts. The hardening is necessary in order to give solid support; if it is lacking, the bones break easily.

Hardening is healthy in the bones. However, hardening is unhealthy in the blood, where it produces arteriosclerosis, and in the vital organs, like the gall bladder and kidneys, where it forms stones. There should be a healthy balance between dissolving and congealing, such as takes place in blood and bone, the two polarities in which the ego is active.

Before indicating further how the activities of Saturn, lead, warmth, and the ego are interrelated and manifest most noticeably with the beginning of the Saturn cycle, an interesting observation can be made. As well as ruling the bones, Saturn rules the body's boundary, the skin. Hence the saying, "only skin and bones" appropriately describes the overactivity of Saturn.

During the incarnating cycles before 21, the soul-spirit principle is unconsciously engrossed in fashioning the body to be its instrument. In the second half of life, when excarnating processes begin and become more evident as we grow older, the astral body and ego are no longer occupied with the upbuilding of the bodily instrument and become freer from it. If the ego is conscious of its spiritual nature and is increasingly our guide, we can grow old in the right way in spite of the fact that mineralizing and cooling processes set in and that our instrument becomes more fragile. For, *lead works rightly if it is controlled by the rejuvenating, Christ-filled ego.*

Aging can be fruitful if ego development ascends while the physical descends. A compensation is thus provided: otherwise, clinging only to the dying, transitory elements—the body and its needs—one is "wrinkled" inwardly as well as outwardly. If the ego exercises no spiritual discipline, then the soul, now freer from the body, tends to exhibit any or many of these negative possibilities: being self-centered, selfish, egotistic, cantankerous, crotchety, miserly, stubborn, insecure, fear-filled, suspicious, cold, unsympathetic, isolated, narrow-minded, bitter, melancholy, despairing, procrastinating, and rutted in the past with its woes, restrictions, failures, and ills.

In the aging and aged, if the spirit-conscious ego guides, reshapes, and fashions the soul in unselfish love and action, the soul becomes more serene, calm, patient, self-controlled, thoughtful, deeply penetrating, secure, prudent, fearless, firm, steadfast, reliable, responsible, and unmoved by vicissitudes except to be prodded to make greater effort to be victorious over them. The goal, then, is to do the will of our Father in heaven and to become perfect as he is perfect.

Perfection is indeed the goal to be attained by all humanity in the remote future, when our highest, but still only germinal spiritual member, the spirit-man, correlated with the Father-principle, will be fully developed through complete transformation of the physical body (see diagram page 87). It is much easier to transform the desires of the astral body into spirit-self, and even relatively easy to change the habits of the etheric body so it becomes life-spirit, than it is to change anything in the dense physical body. Yet we move in that direction when through willed effort, spiritual principles are applied in practical action in the physical world.

Preeminent in such achievement was the way Rudolf Steiner made spiritual science fruitful in every realm of practical life during the years of his Saturn cycle. Here is a brief condensation of these years when the knowledge and the art, born out of the spirit during his Mars and Jupiter cycles, became deed in the Saturn cycle by being applied in solving social tasks and healing social illnesses.[5]

The Saturn cycle in Rudolf Steiner's life

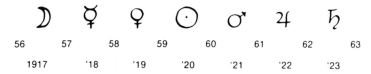

1917, *the Moon year:* Upon request from officials for advice about bringing order out of social chaos, Steiner presented the plan for the Threefold Social Organism. It encountered insufficient grasp of the idea and a lack of creative will. Steiner spoke to large circles on basic truths, and to the prepared on deeper, profound truths. The building, now named the Goetheanum, became a visible monumental work, proving what a practical achievement spiritual science can produce.

1918, *Mercury:* Polarities: at the beginning of the year, retrospect over past changes of consciousness; at the end of the year, outlook on future social duties. These latter ideas were published as a book, *The Threefold Commonwealth,* April 1919. Other polarities: West-East in the earth organism; living and "dead" in the total humanity.

1919, *Venus:* Founding of the First Waldorf School, a living deed in the field of education, based on the life cycles of the developing child. Public eurythmy programs. In the turbulence after the war,

Steiner publicly presented proposals for the Threefold Social Order, with "profoundest inner calm and self-mastery." Many conferences, and conversations with individuals; never a sign of disinclination, only patient listening with understanding and goodness of heart.

1920, the Sun: At Michaelmas, first festival in the auditorium of the Goetheanum, 1,000 present. Opening of the University of Spiritual Science, giving a total world picture, a new synthesis of science, art, religion. Lectures on great individualities in spiritual history. Course for doctors. Attacks from opposers of the new impulses caused added burdens, yet "he continued to advance unconfused toward his goal" of fructifying all areas of life out of spiritual science.

1921, Mars: Severe tests and suffering from vicious accusations. In Stuttgart with 2,500 present, he cleared the air by facing the slanderous untruths with a calm, firm, factual manner, free of emotion. In discussions, "unlimited open-mindedness and patient endurance." Upon request, two theological courses. Opening of the research laboratory at Dornach and the Wegman Clinic in Arlesheim.

1922, Jupiter: Twelve trips abroad in this most expansive year, the peak being the East-West Congress in Vienna where thousands listened intently. Appeal to the capacity of thinking and to broadening horizons of the human spirit. Founding of The Christian Community, a Movement for Religious Renewal. Birth of bio-dynamic agricultural movement. Tragedy of the malicious burning of the Goetheanum on New Year's Eve, yet activities continued unabated January 1st.

1923, Saturn year of Saturn cycle: The sacrificial work of 10 years had been destroyed in one profoundly painful night, but plans were made for a new building made of steel-reinforced concrete, proving the sustaining, upbuilding power of the spirit amid the greatest hindrances and blows of destiny. Insistent retrospection to sift the sound from the unsound. Unshakeable calm and ceaseless effort to awaken souls to assume spiritual and earthly responsibilities, climaxing at Christmas in reorganizing the Anthroposophical Society to be a spiritual community in whose hearts the spiritual Being "Anthroposophy" would have an enduring home in the earthly sphere.

11

THE URANUS CYCLE, 63–70—
NEW WONDERS, UNIVERSALITY

WHATEVER your age, this chapter is for you. Naturally, it will be of the greatest interest to those who have attained or are approaching sixty-three. Yet it is beneficial to see life whole and, through understanding, to be tolerant and sympathetic toward our fellow human beings of all ages.

Within the course of this century, the status of and attitude toward the elderly has changed markedly. Isolation of the aged used to occur mostly in county homes, called "poor houses." Persons not so poor and not so unfortunate were cared for by relatives, often with much love and great respect, and their presence was regarded as a beneficent influence.

Among the factors producing problems for the elderly, and a different attitude toward them, are the lengthening of life expectancy, sky-rocketing costs, and changing life styles. The foundations of family life are less secure, and broken homes are all too prevalent. Space in the home is at a premium, especially in apartments. Nursing and retirement homes have mushroomed, and while some are completely commercial, some sincerely seek to serve the needs of those now called senior citizens. The growing independence of people of all ages—young, middle-aged, and old—readily results in self-interest, and lack of concern for the interests and welfare of others. The glorification of youth and the depreciation of older age creates a waste of most valuable resources of wisdom and fruitful productivity, and casts a blight over what should be the crowning years of life. Basic and most important is the loss of the meaning and purpose of earthlife and its connection with the cosmos.

We have shown how the seven-year cycles unfold under the planetary influences. The inner planetary cycles, Moon, Mercury and Venus, from birth to 21, bring about incarnation into the developing *body*. Enriching life-experience is garnered by the ego working in the sentient, intellectual, and consciousness *soul* during

107

the three Sun cycles, from 21 to 42. Commensurate with one's ability to activate the potentials of the creative *spirit* one contributes to earthlife during the outer planetary cycles, Mars, Jupiter, and Saturn, 42 to 63. We have yet to survey the years beyond 63, when excarnation takes place as the soul and spirit gradually free themselves from the increasingly less vital and less responsive body.

These marvelous processes are summarized in a quotation which you read in the introductory chapter on planetary laws. Within the present context it will now be seen in a new light and be more meaningful: "Together with the earth we exist within seven interpenetrating spheres, and we grow into them, enter into connection with them in the course of life. Our life from birth to death is unfolded out of its inherent tendencies, inasmuch as the star spheres draw us from birth to death. When we have reached the Saturn sphere we have passed through all that the beings of the various planetary spheres in grace accomplish for us, and then, speaking in the occult sense, we enter into a free, moving cosmic existence of our own. It is an existence . . . that can, in a certain sense, be emancipated from what, in the earlier life periods, are still necessities."[1]

> When the Saturn cycle comes to end
> As life proceeds its way to wend,
> A freer, open cycle then begins,
> An intimation of Uranian things.

Some insight can be gained by correlating the free cosmic existence beyond 63 with the transcendental planets beyond Saturn. At the beginning of our cosmic evolution, the present orbit of Saturn was the outermost boundary of planetary development. The origin of the transcendental planets, Uranus, Neptune, and Pluto, was different. From having been comets with eccentric paths, they veered to planetary orbits and joined our planetary system. Evidence of a continuing, diverse, partly non-conforming nature is found in the fact that the axis of Uranus is at nearly a right angle to the axis of the earth, and its moons are retrograde.

Since Saturn, in a way, represents the bounds of time and space, the remote transcendental planets are, in a sense, beyond ordinary time and space. They can be a doorway to higher states of consciousness and supersensible reality, and we may relate them to the excarnating years beyond 63 when we are emancipated from the cosmic necessities of earlier life periods. To Uranus may be assigned the first seven years, 63–70; to Neptune, 70–77; and if the earthlife extends further, then Pluto, 77 onward, although "beyond the norm" is more accurate for Pluto.

The positive expression of Uranus awakens and expands the consciousness—often, like lightning, with flashes of insight. It introduces the new, the unique, and the universal. Universality in one's thinking gives one a cosmic outlook and comprehension, making one a citizen of the cosmos. Universality in one's feelings fosters reverential humility, sympathy, altruism, and brotherhood. Universality in willing sometimes inaugurates and always supports unselfish humanitarian deeds which benefit the totality. The negative side of Uranus is evident in the narrow-minded bigot, the selfish egotist, and the recalcitrant rebel.

Whether one responds positively or negatively to Uranian influences after 63 depends largely on one's destiny background from former lives, on the direction given in the early years of life's unfolding, and on the ego's conscious effort or neglect in purifying the desires, in thinking with clarity, in willingly meeting responsibility, being aware of the spiritual nature of the "I." It also depends on acting courageously and constructively in the Mars cycle, on extending one's outreach and upreach in the Jupiter cycle, and on achieving self-discipline, patience, and stability in the Saturn cycle. The more positively one responds to Uranus, the more easily one can break away from habitual grooves of thinking, feeling, and willing; the more one can free oneself from standardized, rigid routines, the easier it is to adapt oneself to the inevitable, often sudden and unexpected changes that old age brings.

Old age "can be a time of bitter self-absorption, or a time of radiance and blessing," wrote Adam Bittleston.[2] And old age can be all that ranges between these two extremes. Inevitably we grow old. Physiologically we cannot preserve youth. But we can carry from youth into old age something eternally young if we know that in addition to the physical body relating us to the material world, we ourselves and all other selves are spiritual beings connected now with the spiritual world, consciously or unconsciously. After 63, and more so after 70:

> The body may of speed deprive,
> Yet if the spirit is alive,
> The forces of the soul can thrive.

It is the functioning of the soul and spirit that makes the difference, no matter what ills befall the earthly body. With the right
attitude toward one's destiny, it is possible for the spirit to shine
even more brightly in times of adversity. During the last half-year
of his life, Rudolf Steiner, while suffering on a sickbed, worked
without interruption. At tremendous self-sacrifice he gave spiritually to the very last. According to his secretary, "His eyes indicated
the pain he suffered, but they were kinder and more brilliant than
ever."[3]

The Great Physician, the Christ, came to make human beings
"whole." One is whole only when as a spiritual being he relates
rightly to his soul in his physical body. Wholeness is the secret of
maintaining youthfulness in old age and being able to make the
sunset years "a time of radiance and blessing."

The barren intellectualism of our modern culture has developed
intelligence to a high degree, yet lacks spiritual intelligence and
warmth of heart. This has produced generations of human beings
with empty souls, who identify themselves solely with the earthly
body, not knowing that they are in reality spiritual beings. Into
these empty souls the tempters enter with increased force, instill-
ing, on the one hand, egotism, rapacious desires, and bitter discontent, and on the other hand, fear, darkness, insecurity, and
withdrawal. These persons may live a conventional, seemingly
successful life, but, like the foolish virgins in the parable in Matthew 25, they have no "oil" in their lamps when old age comes; they
lack the light of the spirit to guide them triumphantly through whatever sorrows of old age they may experience.

Old age can and should be light-filled, happy, and productive. So
it can be if one stands with awe before the majesty, the mystery,
and the manifold wonders of life. Ever to find something *new* in the
old and familiar is a marvelous means of preserving youthfulness
in old age. By the age of 63 one has awakened nearly 23,000 morn-
ings! For the human being bound by Saturn, the next day will be
"just another day," whereas for the person attuned to Uranus it is
welcomed as "a NEW day." The same applies to each new year as it
unfolds.

The magic of practicing *wonder* was brought to my attention by
this letter from a friend. "Since I last wrote to you about the bout
with cancer and how much help I have had from everyone, especially Dr. Williams and the Lukas Klinik" (Arlesheim, Switzerland), "everything keeps getting better and better, especially my

age, which is 69 years and reveals to me the wonders of growing old."

To my request that she elaborate on "the wonders of growing old," she kindly responded: "For me it is realizing what has been here always. That the earth can produce food and that our bodies can eat the food and make use of it. That we can stand upright and walk. That we have eyes to see and ears to hear the wonders around us. As for the miracle of speech, my great good fortune has been to have speech lessons with Frau Unger-Palmer, during the last four visits I made to the Lukas Klinik. It is just a beginning for me, glimpses of some of the horizons I never dreamed of.

"I realize that all these revelations have appeared because I am alive and well again after the bout with cancer. It's something like a youthfulness that has nothing to do with being young.

". . . My husband has no understanding of Anthroposophy. However, he gives credit to the Lukas Klinik for bringing me through the experience as a happy, grateful, older woman who feels young in spirit. I'm 69 years old."

To friends for their 70th birthday I have sent the following lines which I wrote for my husband when he reached 70.

> Now three-score years and ten
> Have come within your ken;
> From all these scores extract the core
> And find a wealth of rich soul-ore.
>
> Sweet memories recall
> Of times you've sensed the All
> And glimpsed the part you have to play
> In ush'ring in the Coming Day
>
> New strength I pray be thine
> To aid the Powers Divine
> To help mankind to find the way
> To realms where light and love hold sway.

In this series on life's unfolding, it has been indicated that each of the seven-year cycles from birth to 63 is subdivided into seven, a year for each of the successive planets from the Moon to Saturn, with marked characteristics for each one. From 63 to 70, these subdivisions may for some persons continue to have a noticeable effect—they did for me—whereas for others they may be less obvious or even indistinct. The biography of Rudolf Steiner, which was used to illustrate the subdivisions of the Mars, Jupiter, and

Saturn cycles, 42–63, offers no example in the period 63–70, for he died a month after his sixty-fourth birthday. After 63 he said he was free to give certain spiritual revelations which up to that time could not be voiced. What is noteworthy is that far from slackening his pace after 63, he intensified it enormously. During a period of a few weeks he gave 400 personal interviews in addition to four lectures a day. It was as if in this one year were telescoped what another person might experience in many years: all the universality of Uranus, 63–70; the utmost compassion, bestowal, and self-sacrifice of Neptune, 70–77; and finally, the transfiguration of Pluto.

12

THE NEPTUNE CYCLE, 70–77— THE LIFE-SPAN: YEARS OF GRACE, COMPASSION, SELF-BESTOWAL

WHEN the question of age and length of life arose recently on a radio program, the interviewer asked, "Who programs our lives?" The response was, "I don't know." Materialists definitely do not know, and conventional views provide no convincing answers. Health experts and nutritionists make claims that the life-span can be lengthened, some say to 100 and over. Although bad habits may shorten the life expectancy and good habits lengthen it, other factors than the purely physical are at work. Besides having a physical body, every person is a being of soul and spirit; and everyone, although temporarily an earth-dweller, is also a citizen of the cosmos, a member of the great world-organism. Heredity and physical laws affect only the body. The soul is subject to the laws of its self-created destiny. The spirit is governed by the law of repeated earthlives.

Destiny introduces individual variables into the life-span. The destinies of many notable persons, people like Raphael and Mozart, enabled them to contribute immeasurably to human culture in a short life-span, whereas many octogenarians do little more than vegetate. Is there validity in the traditional conception of three-score years and ten? Is it the norm? Is there justice in the programing of the life-spans that undershoot or overshoot the norm? Are there compensations?

Cosmic rhythms enter into the programing. A major rhythm in our solar system is the precession of the equinoxes through all twelve signs of the zodiac in 25,920 years, called the great Platonic cosmic year. By dividing 25,920 by 365.25, we find that a cosmic day is a little over 70 years and 11 months.

It is no chance coincidence that rhythms in our human life correspond to these numbers. We average 18 breaths per minute. Multiplying 18 by 60 minutes per hour, and then the resulting 1,080 by 24 hours per day, we find that we average 25,920 breaths per day, the same number as there are years in a Platonic cosmic year.[1]

Another rhythm that bears a similarity to breathing in and out is our daily waking and sleeping, which signifies that the astral body and ego come in and go out of the physical and etheric bodies. This day and night experience constitutes a "breath" for the living being of the earth. With 365.25 days in a year, when we reach the age of about 70 years and 11 months the earth has had 25,920 such "breaths," and we have lived 25,920 days.

The corresponding numbers in man's breathing rhythm per day, and in the earth's breathing rhythm during man's normal earthly life of nearly 71 years, are identical with those of the much longer cosmic breathing process, for the cosmic day of about 71 years is as a breath in the Platonic cosmic year of 25,920 years. The cosmos "breathes man out" at birth, and about 71 years later "breathes him in" at death. It is this cosmic breathing that programs the normal life-span.

There is also a slightly different way of reckoning. Instead of dividing the 25,920 years of the great Platonic cosmic year by 365.25, the number of days in a year, to arrive at a cosmic day, we can divide 25,920 by 360, the number of degrees in a circle. This gives exactly 72 years, which is the time it takes for the Sun by precession of the equinoxes to move one degree. Rudolf Steiner explained that while the Sun remains over the star in the given degree at one's birth, it strengthens and comforts one, but on moving beyond this star degree, the influence is withdrawn and the earthlife reaches its normal limit. Reverently we should contemplate our relation to the world of the stars and realize that all extension of earthly life beyond 72 is *given by grace*.[2] My lines for friends on their 72nd birthday are:

> Years threescore, ten, and two
> Have now been granted you.
> The future is a gift of grace
> To benefit the human race
> To you I wish today
> A glorious Natal Day!
> I pray this day begins a year
> In which the Living Christ is near,
> Inspiring all you say and do
> And blessing every day anew.

How does the cosmos compensate for a life-span that falls short of or goes beyond the norm? In general, it is true that whoever dies young returns soon to a new earthlife, whereas those who reach a ripe old age must remain much longer in spiritual spheres before reincarnating, that is, remain out of incarnation longer than usual. Rudolf Steiner explained it as follows: Consciousness in the first few years of earthlife is dreamy compared with the consciousness in adult life, which in turn is dark in comparison with the still fuller consciousness in the world of the stars after death. If one dies at 30, the ratio with the first 5 years is 6 to 1; accordingly, one would need to be in the spiritual worlds six times the length of the earthlife.[3] The longer the span of life on the earth, the longer is the span between death and rebirth. From this enormously enlarged view of human life, which an understanding of repeated earthly lives gives, there is no irreparable loss in a short life, nor special merit in an exceptionally long life on the Earth. What is important is that we utilize with utmost responsibility the life-span our destiny allows.

Generalities are less applicable the older one is and the more individualized one becomes. Individual variations prevent the presentation of a predictable pattern. But at 70, and in many instances of earlier retirement, one has reached a peak where at least three possibilities present themselves: (1) to proceed on a plane, leading a routine, rather uneventful existence; (2) to go down a decline where the outlook becomes more and more limited and strength wanes; or (3) to see more peaks ahead toward which one eagerly and resolutely strives. Inasmuch as we are threefold beings, comprised of body, soul, and spirit, it is possible to go in more than one of these directions; that is, the body may decline while the soul and spirit are scaling new heights of illuminated awareness. The body-house may be frail and worn out, but the spirit can be active and the soul be full of life. From the vantage point of 93 years, a wonderfully alert friend observed: "There are surprising compensations in growing old and older. They come quietly in, but there must be many more in the all-pervading cosmic forces if one is open to them. It seems, in a sense, like a reviewing of one's life and a grasping of the core of each experience as it comes."

How we meet old age depends largely on the degree of our spiritual development and on how we lived through the earlier stages of life. As an example of the latter, Rudolf Steiner stated: "The qualities absorbed in early life reappear in a remarkable way in old age. When a child has absorbed a great deal of rightly guided devotion, the latter becomes in old age strength for a life of activity. Strength is the quality manifested in old age as the outcome of devotion cultivated in youth. A childhood void of religiousness and love will develop into a weak and powerless old age."[4] Bending the knees in childhood brings new force into the legs. By clasping the hands in devotion, the ego is enlivened and a new force flows through the heart, kindles love, and in old age bestows on the hands the power to bless. The head bowed in devotion likewise gains a new force.

In the early cycles of life, the self was entering earthlife and establishing itself in the bodily instrument. In the late cycles, especially after 70, the soul and spirit loosen from the body and gradually excarnation takes place. If one responds positively to Neptune during the Neptune cycle, 70–77, one can be attuned to the divine, be inwardly tranquil and at peace, and be a blessing to others. A negative response to Neptune presents a tragic figure: confused, forgetful, bewildered, chaotic.

As in the Uranus cycle, 63–70, freshness is maintained by *wonder* that not only sees the new in the new but more importantly finds something new in the familiar, so in the Neptune cycle after 70, genuine humanness and beautiful blossoms of life appear when *compassion* comes to the fore. On the one hand, no longer need one prove oneself, assert oneself, or promote personal interests, and on the other hand, one should not harden within oneself, withdraw in loneliness, drift into dull aimlessness, or feel abandoned and rejected. Without loss of ego-identity, in complete inner freedom, one can unselfishly relate to others, compassionately enter into their feelings, sense their needs, and out of one's mature wisdom, love, self-surrender, self-sacrifice, and willing renunciation—some of the finest fruits of Neptune—provide an uplifting and healing influence. Then these years can be golden sunset years.

However, if one has throughout life been selfishly oriented, it will be difficult to make the transition from "mine" to "thine" as one advances from the previous cycles of necessity to the universality of life of the transcendental planets, Uranus, Neptune, and Pluto. Whoever maintains a mine-attitude will find life increasingly limited, restricted, cramped, and closing in on one, whereas for one who has the thine-attitude, life opens out in increasing wonderment during the Uranus cycle; and through *compassion* in the Neptune cycle, one is set free from oneself, transcends one's own I, passes beyond oneself into the joys and sufferings of others, and in some instances, into supersensible experiences.[5] Neptune signifies a unity which transcends the individual and a reaching out to infinity, which can be done safely provided one's own individuality is well established.

The Twelve Senses

Transcendence of the physical and personal can be applied beneficially in connection with the twelve senses, not waiting until 70, but beginning already at 63. One characteristic of aging is the weakening of the sense organs. Instead of fretting over any loss of their functioning, life can be enriched if their processes are elevated to a soul-spirit level. To illustrate this, here are brief examples based on the excellent book, *The Fulfillment of Old Age*,[6] which Dr. Norbert Glas wrote out of his rich experience—his prolonged study of Anthroposophy, his long medical practice, and operating a nursing home for the elderly. "Glas' book," wrote a friend over 70, "is a kind of bible for me. I turn to it often in stress."

Sight. The eye establishes harmony by producing a complementary color. To apply this to the soul, develop the inner vision to "see" the wisdom and justice of events of destiny, especially of the failures, reverses, misfortunes. Accept them as needed experience, be grateful for all lessons learned, and peacefully, without regrets, recognize that destiny is always a friend. *Hearing.* Listen with the soul, listen silently, selflessly, with full attention, without criticism. Hear what things themselves are saying. *Smell.* Never "turn up the nose," shunning contact with fellow human beings, but with compassion and love, sense the true essence of others.

Taste. Indulge not in insult or whatever leaves "a bad taste"; develop courtesy. *Touch.* Overcome egotistic curiosity and "touch-all" inquisitiveness; touch things with reverence; play musical instruments and develop skill with handcrafts. *Warmth.* Cultivate patience, great warmth of heart, an ardent soul, and fiery spirit.

Balance. Inner tranquillity and equilibrium. *Life.* Evenness of temper and service benefiting others. *Movement.* Despite physical limitations, rejoice in inner freedom; for example, when my husband could no longer go for walks, he contentedly settled in a chair and read books on travel, on birds, on spiritual science, etc.

Speech. Sense the divine power of the word; be courageous. *Thought.* Avoid excessive talkativeness; be silent within, be contemplative, and assimilate new ideas. *Ego-sense.* Go beyond appearances, sense the ego of others and consider the interest of others as much as your own.

Even when older age becomes somewhat burdensome, the light-filled soul aims to be not a burden but a blessing.

13

THE PLUTO CYCLE, BEYOND THE NORM—
CONSCIENCE, TRANSFIGURATION

WONDER awakens the urge to reach out beyond ourselves and beyond the physical world. Compassion likewise enables us to transcend our own "I," to go beyond outer impressions and to gain insight into the world of a fellow human being. This we should strive to do throughout life, but the time when we can best transcend ourselves and our previous powers of wonder and compassion is when life's unfolding takes us beyond the spheres of necessity that end with the Saturn cycle at 63, and we enter the freer spheres of what are called the transcendental planets, Uranus and Neptune, whose orbits are beyond the orbit of Saturn.

The Uranus cycle, 63–70, can be a wonderful period if we marvel at the endless new wonders we can encounter daily. After 70, during the Neptune cycle, when the excarnating process increases apace, we can more easily transcend ourselves, pour forth selfless love, and willingly make self-sacrifices.

The third transcendental planet is Pluto, discovered in 1930. Pluto's orbit is highly eccentric. Unlike the orbits of the other planets, Pluto's orbit is slanted far above and far below the ecliptic. It is relatively narrow and greatly elongated, sometimes even going inside the orbit of Neptune and at other times very far distant. The speed of Pluto's movement is remarkably variable, ranging from 13 to 32 years in one sign of the zodiac, but averaging about 24 years.

What do these "gestures" of the planet Pluto reveal concerning its role in life's unfolding? It certainly cannot be assigned a seven-year period, nor can we strictly say that its sphere of influence begins at 77 and extends indefinitely to death. Cannot we sometimes see it already active in the Neptune cycle, especially in the years of grace after 72? And as ruler of death, Pluto can strike at any age. The most accurate designation seems to be to relate it to "beyond the norm," in terms of years. One characteristic of Pluto is that it carries on further beyond the usual limits, beyond the normal boundaries.

Pluto has been called the arch-extremist.[1] This is because, on the one hand, it can carry one to lofty heights of spirituality, beyond Imagination (spiritual seeing), beyond Inspiration (spiritual hearing), to Intuition (union with spiritual Beings).[2] On the other hand, it can debase and lead to depths of degradation. In old age one is not likely to become a criminal, but in our times the elderly have become prime victims of crime. The greater the challenges, the greater is the need to rise to higher spiritual capacities.

Pluto invariably presents the elderly—each according to his destiny—with some of the following challenging experiences: change compelling adjustment and transformation; elimination of the effete, of all that has served its purpose and become useless; values to be examined for reevaluation; priorities to be scrutinized and shifted; limitations to be transcended; handicaps to be overcome; habit patterns due for refashioning; conscience prompting restitution; wrong that must be righted; truth to be translated into purposeful action; drastic upheaval necessitating revision; patience and endurance tried by excruciating pain; tranquillity tested by disruptions; dissolution demanding solution; destruction requiring re-creation; death transfigured by rebirth.

In a recent radio interview, a youthful amputee was asked how one reacts to the loss of a limb. Her instant and emphatic reply was, "It depends on what you were before." If the question is asked as to how one reacts to aging, the answer is the same, "It depends on what you were before." Relatively few elderly persons lose a limb, yet there are other eventual, inevitable losses and necessary adjustments. In accord with individual destiny, they vary in kind and degree, from the loss of speed, to complete disability and the loss of loved ones.

It may be helpful to refer briefly to the least of these—loss of speed. This may appear to some to be trivial, yet it is perhaps the most universal. When I was in my 60s, a friend in her 70s used to affirm repeatedly what an elderly woman had told her years before, namely, that after 70, every year slackens one's pace much more than one ever anticipated it would. Now that I am in my mid-70s, I realize the truth of that statement more than I was able to formerly.

Simple things like dressing in the morning and having breakfast take longer than they used to. In order not to be delayed in leaving home when I have an appointment, I prepare in advance all that I

need to take with me, else the last minutes pass like seconds and I
would not be ready on time. Someone a little older than I am
mentioned her difficulty in keeping pace with all of her former
activities, as well as those of her husband—it really was wearing
her down. In my reply I must have mentioned my own problem of
facing the need to willingly sacrifice some things. Her answer was a
positive expression of earnest striving to diminish quantity but not
quality.

The amputee in the aforementioned interview enumerated three
things that were most helpful to her: a sense of humor, determina-
tion, and the support of family and friends. It is important for young
people to understand the last statement. They may be decades
away from old age but, with right understanding of how life unfolds, they can give helpful support to the elderly, rather than being
impatient or shunning them. Someone who had felt hurt, because a
friend had seemed indifferent toward her shortly before he died,
was greatly relieved when the excarnation process was explained.
She then realized that the soul and spirit were no longer fully
present and in command of the body.

How aging persons learn to live with losses and limitations depends largely on their richness of soul and confidence in the spirit.
In 2 Corinthians 4:16, St. Paul aptly described how it can be done,
"Though our outer nature is wasting away, our inner nature is
being renewed every day."

Without this daily inner renewal from spiritual sources, and without previous self-discipline, one might complain about physical
disabilities as did an 85-year-old novelist in a cleverly written article, "My Crabbéd Age." She abhorred and designated as balder-
dash the famous lines of Robert Browning:

> Grow old along with me!
> The best is yet to be,
> The last of life, for which the first was made.
> Our times are in His hand
> Who saith, "A whole I planned;
> Youth shows but half. Trust God; see all,
> nor be afraid!"[3]

She said she would like to be 35 again, yet know at that age what
she has learned since. "What I mind is not my age but the insistence
that all is sweetness and light as one rides off into the sunset—
or, more accurately, stumbles downhill. I dislike the handicaps, the

figurative straitjacket, the destruction of mobility, the lessening of sight. . . . I know that I cannot alter my physical disabilities, so I'll live with them—but I don't have to like it. And I do have one regret. There are so many people I'd like to meet, so many places I'd like to see."[4] This one regret would be obviated had she the enlarged view that repeated earthlives give.

I receive many letters attesting to joy in the Pluto years despite serious handicaps. Each individual has the choice of responding to the rebellious nature of Pluto or to its transfiguring influence. Confined to her isolated home in the country, an elderly friend wrote that instead of being a prisoner, she had chosen to be "a happy hermit." At 82, a man who for years had cared for his invalid wife stated: "I do as well as I can. I've had to give up much that I'd like to do, but I'm resigned to this and must respect my age and be sensible about it."

A year ago, at the age of 79, a New Jersey friend was in a car crash in New England. Here is part of her letter: "It was truly a miracle that I came off with my life and injuries that can be repaired. . . . To be utterly helpless and dependent on others is something new to me and a lesson in patience. Since I am home I had an astral vision of the event, the whole thing, and I can say the Heavenly Forces certainly were present—never to be forgotten. I am determined to be cooperative in every way—to mitigate and heal whatever karma has to be worked out. . . . But when I reached home another major shock confronted me—the incredible unkindness and inhumanness of my (relative). It is something that puzzles me. I hope it is a test for me spiritually and I am treating it so.

"I am aware of the constructive possibilities in this picture and I am invoking the Great Ones' help in what . . . I wish to be worked out. Of course this is not for the immediate situation but probably more to establish a foundation for a future life. . . . One must never lose sight of the fact that the life of Jesus—the physical events—reflect what spiritually the soul must experience on the great journey toward Christhood."

At nearly 93, a blind friend still lives alone and never utters a complaint. She is always cheerful and wants to be helpful to others. In her 89th year, another beautiful soul, both blind and deaf and living in a rest home, asked a friend to write me these lines: "God has provided a happy situation in my aloneness and twilight years, so my heart overflows with gratitude." Another friend, now 90, with only 10 percent vision because of inoperable "gray veils" before her eyes, and shut in for months, alone, due to a fall, wrote on a Christmas card: "I know my Lord does not allow one of His children to experience such an ordeal without having a definite plan to bring great blessing out of the difficulties. I am still able to thank Him for the storms as well as for the calms, so can live as happily content as I did before the storm. And to God be the glory for that. What a sweet discipline pain is! My days are *good* days even when they are *bad* days." In her autobiography, Martha Humbard states, "All the dirt, grime, sweat, and sawdust comes back as a sweet fragrance in my memory, for the years have a way of smoothing out the rough edges and taking away the bitterness."[5]

The Pluto years do have the power to transfigure experiences and transfigure our souls. When speaking about old age, someone whose views I respect commented that an exceptionally long life, far beyond the norm, may be granted in order to bring about forgiveness and reconciliation. Not until then are some persons able to transcend the misunderstandings, egotism, and hatred of the past, and to listen to the voice of conscience. As Uranus arouses wonder, and as Neptune deepens compassion, so *Pluto intensifies conscience*—our inner prompter which helps us to judge right from wrong.

In mythology, Pluto is presented as an incorruptible, just judge. The power of judging was then still outside the soul. As the coming of Christ approached, this power passed from outside to inside the soul, and conscience was born. Conscience is that divine power within, which leads us beyond our likes and dislikes, beyond pleasure and displeasure. It enables us to transcend our desires, passions, urges, and selfish impulses.[6] It strengthens us to fulfill our moral responsibilities and obligations. It is our inner corrector. It has nothing to do with utility.[7] It attests that there is a reality that transcends the physical world, that transcends, too, the dark underworld of Hades (Pluto). It gives evidence of a supersensible spiritual world. It is a holy, inviolable possession. Its highest manifestation comes from moral insight.

Beginning in our era, conscience will more and more become a presentiment prophetically revealing how we shall experience the consequences of our deeds in the future and after death.[8] All reconciliation has to take place, however, on the earth, either in this or a future earthlife. If souls were only aware of how they burden themselves by clinging to hate and enmity; if they were only aware of what joy it is to have a clear conscience, to have a mind and heart filled with peace and love—love even for one's enemies.

"Where there is hatred, let me sow love," prayed St. Francis. "It is in pardoning that we are pardoned; it is in dying that we are reborn to Eternal Life." If our conscience has been active, and if, like St. Paul, we can say, "I die daily" (1 Corinthians 15:31), by the time we reach the Pluto years we have cast off, have "died" to, our undesirable qualities of soul and given up impeding possessions, then we can approach the portal of death fearlessly, unencumbered, transfigured through conscious, free spiritual activity, and bearing a maximum of invisible spiritual fruit (Galatians 5:22).

14

THE PORTAL OF DEATH

OF ALL fears that beset mankind, one of the most intense and universal is the fear of death. It has not always been so, for our relation to death has undergone a change. In ancient times we were more conscious of the spiritual world than of the physical world, hence when the physical body was vacated, there was no experience of death as we know it today. In proportion as our connection with the spirit faded and the physical body became more important, death was increasingly dreaded, until in our era in the Western world, consciousness of the spirit and soul has been for a large number completely lost and the body has become all-important. When human beings identify themselves solely with the body, no wonder there is such fear of death.

But now the tide is turning. In recent years there has arisen a growing interest in thanatology, the science of death, pioneered by Dr. Elizabeth Kübler-Ross.[1] Death education is a rapidly growing field of study, teaching, and counseling, giving new meaning to life as well as an understanding of death and dying. This new field is beginning to be regarded as a healing art, as having therapeutic value. And so indeed it does. It diminishes the immense fear surrounding death.

Another significant contribution to lifting this fear was made in 1975 when Dr. Raymond A. Moody, Jr., presented authentic experiences of clinical death.[2] His first book, *Life after Life*, quickly became a best seller, and was soon followed by a sequel.[3] The many testimonies of meeting the Christ, the Being of ineffable light and love, fulfills Rudolf Steiner's prophetic statement early in this century that from the 1930s onward, more and more people would see the Christ in etheric form—the true second coming—and that in the course of the twentieth century Christ would become the Lord of Destiny (Karma), meeting souls at the portal of death and determining how individual destiny can best serve the collective progress of humanity.[4] All fear is removed and joy takes its place as one glimpses the glorious prospects for the gradual transfiguration of all mankind through repeated deaths and rebirths till the mortal takes on immortality. Steiner stated it thus:

> All things alive throughout the Universe
> Live but in bringing forth within them
> The seed of a new life.
> So too the soul of Man is given up
> To aging and to death,
> Only that deathless he may ripen
> To ever newly resurrected life.[5]

In "Gareth and Lynette," a section of *Idylls of the King,* Alfred Lord Tennyson pictures "The war of time against the soul of man." After conquering the three warriors, Morning-Star, Noon-Sun, and Evening-Star, Gareth was confronted by:

> A huge man-beast of boundless savagery,
> He names himself the Night and oftener Death.

Over his helmet was a skull. Gareth split the skull and then the helmet.

> . . . . And out from this
> Issued the bright face of a blooming boy
> Fresh as a flower new-born . . . .
>
>   Then sprang the happier day from underground;
> And Lady Lyonors and her house, with dance
> And revel and song, made merry over Death,
> As being after all their foolish fears
> And horrors only proven a blooming boy.
> So large mirth lived and Gareth won the quest.[6]

One need not hesitate to use the word "death," for it is as much a part of life as is birth. It is not true to say there is no death. What is true is that death does not end life; it ends merely our temporary life on the earth. The physical body dies, but the soul and spirit enter worlds of soul and spirit. Steiner therefore nearly always spoke of "the gate of death" or "the portal of death." "Portal" enables us at once to picture not an end but a stately entrance. Before we ourselves pass through the portal of death, we experience the death of friends and relatives.

What I learned when my husband passed through the portal of

death has been helpful to many persons. Life shared with another brings about an interweaving of the life forces of the etheric bodies. When the one etheric body is withdrawn at death, it leaves what is comparable to rents, tears, or gaps in the etheric body of the person left on the earth. This is what causes the grief, loneliness, and emptiness, more than does the absence of the physical presence. For the average person it may take three years to heal these disrupted etheric forces. I was extremely grateful that the exalted spiritual atmosphere of my husband John's funeral service effected an instantaneous healing. The three days following his death had been agonizing, but after the healing, I experienced bliss. During the night after the funeral I awakened rejoicing, for there was nothing but joy at the vivid realization that human beings are spiritual beings and the world is filled with spirit.

A few months later when friends from Florida visited me, I think they were shocked that I laughed so much. But I knew that John wanted me to be joyous, and that my joy gave joy to him, whereas had I grieved it would have grieved him. It is most helpful to those who have passed through the portal of death if we feel only gratitude for all they meant to us, instead of grieving that they are no longer with us. When loved ones depart, our power to love remains. Love and gratitude build the bridge between the visible and invisible worlds, and enable the loved one in the supersensible spiritual world to:

Live, borne by love
Blessed by light, upwards.[7]

Consciousness of our connection with our loved ones and their continued gaze on us can strengthen our conscience and be a moral influence. This I know from experience. At the age of four, I was present when my maternal grandmother passed through the portal of death. Thereafter she was a monitor of my conduct. I remember saying to myself, "Grandma does not want me to do that," or "Grandma wants me to do this."

In innumerable ways, those on the other side of the threshold are far more helpful to us than we ever imagine, or normally become consciously aware of. Sometimes a parent who dies confers upon his or her offspring the special talents which the parent had not been able to make fruitful, as did the father of Raphael.[8] Or a mother may, after sufficient sojourn in the soul world, supply youthful forces to her adult daughter. A close cooperation may exist between persons on the earth and those in a higher world, resulting in phenomenal and even quite miraculous achievements.

During the last half-year I have been notified of the death of more than a dozen friends, five of them in one week. That is exceptional, yet it focuses on the realization that as one advances in years, one is more frequently faced with the reality of death. As more and more of one's contemporaries pass through the portal of death, and one is oneself steadily approaching that portal, what may have formerly seemed a thick wall becomes a thin veil. With many of one's loved ones "there," the "there" and "here" become more and more unified. An eighty-year-old friend wrote me recently that many years ago an elderly close friend "used to often mention the time of passing and I didn't want her to, but now I realize it is a marvelous thing to look forward to, yet ever keeping your feet plainly fixed on earth."

It is realistic and not the least bit morbid to make specific preparations for one's departure— just as realistic as it is to prepare a layette before a child is born. For example, one should have a certified will, and leave instruction for the care of the body and for the last rites. Nowadays it might be wise to make it clear that one wishes to be allowed to cross the portal of death naturally, without artificially prolonging life—a cruelty comparable to preventing a child from being born.

It is wise to request that there be no embalming—dry ice or a sealed casket can be used—and that the body be kept in a quiet atmosphere for at least three days, while the life-forces gradually withdraw, before cremation. Unfortunately the trend lately has been toward having no funeral, not realizing the great importance to the soul and spirit if the entry into the higher worlds is accompanied with due reverence and love, and with the aid of spiritual Beings, as occurs in the Christian Community ritual. The service should be a solemn festival, free from sadness, establishing the right relation between the sense-perceptible and supersensible realms.

These are practical arrangements that can be made well in advance, but the inner attitudes, too, are essential and should be of prime concern in the later years of life's unfolding. One of these attitudes is detachment from things, for possessions all too often possess us. Some souls strongly attached to earthly things remain earthbound after death. I was delighted when my parents, entirely on their own initiative, announced after their golden wedding anniversary that they were selling their house and would rent the ground floor of a two-family house adequate for their needs.

One of my friends, who toward the close of earthlife had to give up housekeeping to enter a home for the elderly, was loath to part from her silver and the other possessions to which she was attached. She acted on the suggestion that instead of regretting that she had to part from them, she have only gratitude for the privilege of their use so many years. In this way she was able to make the transition joyously. Clinging to things of sense, and with the soul encumbered with hatred, enmity, bitterness, resentment, and self-pity, one cannot pass through the portal of death peacefully. Blessed is the soul who is nourished and sustained by the spirit, and who loves his neighbor as himself, and hence can cross the portal between the earthly and supersensible realms consciously and joyously.

One who was present when Rudolf Steiner consciously drew his last breath described the atmosphere as being not that of an end but of "a most sublime spiritual action," no cessation of consciousness but an exalted, transfigured wakefulness. His "countenance spoke of peace, grace, inner certitude, spiritual vision" as he entered into "worlds of life and action."[9]

The supreme example of facing death with sublime equanimity is narrated in the gospels, particularly chapters 14 through 17 of the Gospel of St. John. Remember that these words about peace, love, joy, comfort, and good cheer were spoken, not by someone in ripe old age, but at the age of thirty-three, fully conscious that it was the eve of his ignominious crucifixion. "Let not your heart be troubled . . . . Peace I leave with you, my peace I give unto you: not as the world giveth, give I unto you. Let not your heart be troubled, neither let it be afraid" (John 14:1,27).

If it is possible at the moment of death, one should picture oneself walking up a hill from which the Christ is walking down to greet one. Then one enters not night and darkness but the supernal Light of the Christ when one passes through the portal of death.

At the conclusion of *Life's Unfolding from Conception to Death,* it is appropriate to repeat the quotation given in the chapters on planetary laws and on the Mars cycle: "Seldom nowadays do we find people with gray hair and wrinkles welcoming with joy the dawn of each year because each year brings new possibilities of development to the organism, and new knowledge unattainable before is within reach. . . . We should actually retain the possibility, all through life, of rejoicing in the coming year, because each year charms forth the divine-spiritual content of our own inner being in ever new forms.

"I want to emphasize this point. We should really and truly learn to experience our life as capable of development not only in youth, but through the whole span between birth and death."[10]

The portal of death, in turn, leads to tremendous tasks as we journey through the cosmos between death and rebirth, amid the sublime activity of the ranks of the Spiritual Hierarchies described in Part II. In the worlds of soul and of spirit we behold our life on the earth in new perspective and prepare the spirit-germ for the next earthly life. We enter earthly life with the prenatal will to carry out our destiny and to garner new fruits as life unfolds, cycle after cycle, and year after year. If we work diligently toward our self-perfecting, without self-seeking, not only do we leave a richer legacy on the earth, but the more do we promote the entire cosmic evolution of mankind, as conscious and conscientious *citizens of the cosmos.*

PART II

Our Journey Through the Cosmos Between Death and Rebirth

"In my Father's house are many mansions"

15

OVERCOMING BARRIERS TO
SPIRITUAL UNDERSTANDING

AN ESSENTIAL factor of life is rhythm. All of us are experiencing it this moment in our breathing. Inhaling and exhaling in breathing constitute a rhythm whereby we are revitalized. A larger rhythm is that of waking and sleeping. Through this alternating rhythm we are refreshed. There is also the rhythm of the seasons which gives renewal to all life on the earth. Another rhythm that covers a much longer span of time is that of earthlife and spherelife, a sojourn on earth followed by a journey through the planetary spheres of the cosmos. As in sleep we are refreshed, so through this cosmic journey we are refashioned by the forces of the cosmos as our destiny permits; the ancients called it "being made young again."

The title of Part II implies rhythm. If it were worded, "Our Journey After Death," no rhythm would be involved. Stating it as "Our Journey Through the Cosmos Between Death and Rebirth" implies that we have a "round-trip ticket." It is like a larger breathing rhythm, exhaling the soul and spirit into the cosmos, then inhaling them into a new physical body for a new earthlife. That is how it appears from the human viewpoint on earth. From the viewpoint of the cosmos it is reversed. The cosmos breathes us out at earthly birth; it breathes us in when we pass through the portal of death.

Interest in reincarnation is growing rapidly. However, if people have not dematerialized and spiritualized their thinking, they are apt to think of reincarnation primarily or wholly in terms of the earthlife, with no concept of what happens in the cosmos between death and rebirth. Our experiences in the cosmos between incarnations are very important. Few souls, as yet, know anything about what happens in realms of soul and spirit among the exalted Beings of the Spiritual Hierarchies. If reincarnation is regarded only in terms of repeated lives on earth without interim periods in the cosmos, it presents a materialistic and egotistic outlook, encompassing only the earthly and the personal, and omitting that which is cosmic and spiritual.

In recent centuries materialism has, figuratively speaking, erected a wall between the physical world and the worlds of soul and spirit. There is good purpose, however, for the wall having been erected. The purpose is this: by being alienated from the spiritual world, man developed his own ego consciousness and freedom. Benefit has been derived from the wall, yet at a large price. For many people the price is emptiness of soul, because physical life alone cannot satisfy the soul. And think of the great amount of grief, sorrow, fear, and insecurity that is experienced because people think that death is the end of life. Think of the mourning connected with death. This is the price for the wall having been erected. Once the wall is removed, vast vistas open, mourning is alleviated, and life is enriched enormously. It is like getting out of a prison cell and feeling the expanses of the universe. We feel ourselves no longer bounded by our skin; we realize more fully, in greater reality, that we are indeed cosmic beings; we are *citizens of the cosmos.*

Attempts are being made today to break through the wall, one means being extrasensory perception (ESP). Increasing numbers of people are trying to crack the wall to get insights into what is on the other side. Many young people want to understand what life is about and to know more than they have been taught. Some of them are born knowers. [Since this was written many years ago, marked strides have been taken in this direction, as already noted in "The Portal of Death," the last chapter of Part I, Life's Unfolding.]

Sometimes life-experiences bring an awakening. I have friends who had two children. One was a little girl who was subject to asthma. Whenever she had an attack, her mother used a certain procedure to help her get over it. One day when the children were playing outside, the little girl, then six years old, felt the approach of an attack and went into the house. When the mother started the usual procedure, the child said to her, "You do not need to do that, Mother. My Angel says I am not going to stay." The mother could hardly believe what she heard. The child repeated it, "My Angel says I am not going to stay." Peacefully she died. This experience prompted the parents to search for explanations and thus they came to Anthroposophy. They had to have satisfactory answers to the questions which such a life-experience awakened in them.

Sometimes the death of a loved one in war or in an accident

makes a window in the wall, and one begins to realize the need for and the possibility of comprehending what is on the other side. It was materialistic science that erected the wall. Philosophy contributed, too, by setting limits to verifiable knowledge, claiming, with Kant, that one can know only so much, beyond which it is impossible to go. That has been the accepted viewpoint. Spiritual science tears down, dissolves, the wall. With scientific exactness it describes the worlds of soul and spirit, their relation to the physical world, and the long journey we take through those worlds between death and rebirth to a new life on earth.

A journey can be described in detail or briefly. If someone spent the summer in Europe and talked to you about it for an hour, you would learn a little, but far from all that occurred. Similarly, the journey through the cosmos that takes centuries cannot be explained in detail in one hour. We can get only some glimpses that will give us a better idea of it. One can describe different aspects of a journey: the places, the people, the customs. So in describing the cosmic journey we can speak of the various realms through which we pass, the different relationships we have with other human beings and with the hierarchical Beings above man, and the activities that occur in the spiritual spheres.

If one were even briefly to describe the earth, a true picture would not be presented unless one included the poles and the tropics as well as the temperate zones; not only land masses, but also the oceans; not one continent, but all the continents; the Orient as well as the Occident; the mountains and the plains; the cities and the rural areas. One must take into account the variety. Descriptions of higher worlds must likewise include all the realms, beginning with the Moon sphere and extending to the zodiac. For indeed, "In my Father's house are many mansions" (John 14:2). Misconceptions arise when one mistakes a part for the whole.

At the same time one should be ever mindful of the connection between the earth and those realms. One can think of the two aspects of existence—the earthlife and the cosmic spherelife—as resembling one's two hands. This is an apt illustration in several ways. Place your hands together, one above the other. You see that your two hands are two halves which are opposite yet identical, and they fit each other. Your hands are different from all others. Of course, there is a similarity in hands, yet no two pairs are alike. If you tried to match one of your hands with another person's hand, the two would not fit as do your own two hands. This principle is applicable in our description of what happens between incarnations. One can give certain generalizations about the journey through the cosmos, yet for each human being it is to some extent an individual experience. Your own earthlife and spherelife relate to each other as do your own two hands. What we are on earth determines what our spherelife will be, and that in turn conditions the next earthlife.

We might think of the relationship between earthlife and spherelife as comparable to a photo with its negative and positive, one being the reverse of the other, yet they belong together. Likewise, every thought, every feeling, and every deed on earth has a counterpart in the worlds of soul and spirit.

One difficulty that arises when one wants to describe other worlds is that of language. Our languages apply to earth experience; they are not adapted to the spiritual world. If a bird could speak, imagine it trying to tell a cow what it means to fly! Whenever something is beyond our experience, new concepts and new terminology must be developed if there is to be communication and understanding. New concepts have to be introduced if we are to try to clothe in earthly language what the experiences in the spiritual world are.

Recently I had to go somewhere by taxi. The taxi driver went through a section of Brooklyn, New York, that I had not seen before. I made the comment that I had never been in that part of the city. He said, "Well, see all you can, lady. The time will come when you won't see a thing." With this lecture in mind, I said, "I expect to see very much, even more than on the earth; of course, not with physical eyes, nor will there be physical objects." He replied, "If that is what you believe, I hope it is true." I answered, "It is more than a belief; it is something about which one can know and have conviction, if one truly is aware that man is more than just body—that he is body, soul, and spirit. Of course the body dies, but if there is soul and spirit, then there is something beyond death." That was as far as he could go and the subject was dropped.

The crux of the whole thing is in the nature of man and the nature of the universe. According to spiritual science, there is not only the physical world, but also the soul world and the spiritual world. Between the physical world and the soul and spiritual worlds is what we referred to as the wall. The wall was successfully erected by materialism, Relating this to man, everyone knows that man has a physical body; but he also has a soul, and he has a spirit. Many people think of themselves as body only, thereby erecting the wall within their consciousness. (The diagram, presented in a spatial sense, indicates how the realms are kept apart in consciousness, whereas, in fact, they interpenetrate one another.)

spiritual world	spirit
soul world	soul
physical world	body

The wall separating the physical world from the soul and spiritual worlds

Science, particularly medical science, has done a great deal to describe the body. It has added enormously to our information about it. As for the soul, what does psychology know about the soul? The word psychology itself means the science of the soul. Usually the soul is related to the body as if it were not an entity in itself but dependent on the body, even character traits being linked with the bodily and chemical processes. Moreover, psychologists do not go beyond one earthlife. They try to go back to early memories; however, they have no inkling of what lies before birth and of what the ego brings with it as its own self-created destiny from previous incarnations.

As for the spirit, in the year 869 A.D. there was, as previously mentioned, a council in which the church fathers decreed that henceforth it would be heretical to speak of man as part spirit; he was to be recognized as body and soul only. To this day some still cling to this tenet. If we know we are spirit as well as soul and body, we think for ourselves instead of accepting church dogma on authority. Man's loss of consciousness of his spirit nature was a necessary part of the evolutionary process. It had to occur. Man had to experience total materialism in order to become *self*-conscious and to master the outer world. We have come so far, however, that some churchmen themselves do not believe in the spirit. And some who do believe in a supersensible world think of it as having only two realms, heaven and hell, distinctly separate, which subject one to everlasting bliss or damnation.

Spiritual science recognizes that man is body, soul, and spirit, that in addition to the physical world, there is a soul world and a spiritual world, and it shows our relationship to those worlds. Spiritual science is not to be confused with spiritualism, which tries to bring an excarnated spirit to manifestation in the physical world. Nor is it a mysticism that lifts one more or less out of the body into a spiritual realm where one is apt to lose one's own identity as a self-conscious and individual human being. Nor is the science of the spirit, as given by Rudolf Steiner, something brought over from the East. While explaining the East and appreciating its spirituality, it is not a transplanted Eastern teaching. It is presented in the form needed in the twentieth century. If you want to know about Europe and ask someone to tell you about it, you do not expect him to tell you how Europe was in the Middle Ages, or earlier; you want him to tell you how it is now. At least here in the Western world we want to know what is suitable for the intellectualized and individualized man in our age of technology. In our Western spiritual world-conception, the Christ-impulse is central and foremost.

Information on the science of the spirit, or Anthroposophy, is amply available. There are many books and thousands of printed lectures by Rudolf Steiner, a foremost scientist of the supersensible. Some of his books and lecture cycles relating to our cosmic journey between death and rebirth are listed in the "Notes" section.

16

AT THE DEPARTURE GATE

To AVOID the word death, some people use expressions such as "passing on," or "transition." Some maintain, "There is no death." There *is* death, but death does not end life. We should recognize that death is an actual experience, as is birth. Just as truly as we speak of birth, we can rightly speak of death; we need not hedge around it. Rudolf Steiner, whose supersensible sight enabled him to describe the event, did not evade the word death, yet he seldom used it alone; he usually said, "the gate of death," or "the portal of death." It does help a great deal if we say gate of death, because a gate implies that there is something beyond, that it is not a "dead end." The gate of death leads from earthlife to spherelife. The gate enables us to pass from this limited world of space and time into cosmic vastness and ever-changing consciousness.

In order to understand what happens at death we must differentiate more than body, soul, and spirit, for each of these, in turn, is threefold. Our concern now is with the body, which can be differentiated as physical body, etheric body, and astral body. Minerals have only a physical body. Plants have something more, an etheric body, also called the life body or body of formative forces, giving life and growth. Animals likewise have a physical and a life body and, in addition, they have an astral or soul body that gives feeling and voluntary movement. Man is not an animal, for besides the physical, etheric, and astral bodies, he has an ego, or "I," which gives *self*-consciousness, thus raising man into a kingdom above the animal.

The etheric or life body remains with the physical body as long as one has not yet passed through the gate of death. The physical and the etheric remain together day and night throughout earthlife, whereas every time we go to sleep, the astral body and the ego separate from the physical and the etheric. Sleep is called the little brother of death because in both sleep and death the soul and spirit are lifted out; while sleep and death differ from each other in that at

death the etheric body also withdraws. As long as the etheric body
remains with the physical, as it does in sleep, there is life in the
physical body. When the etheric also withdraws, there is left only
the physical body, which is then a corpse, merely a shell, subject to
the laws of the physical world. When the physical body is no longer
maintained by the life forces, its elements return to the physical
earth, either by decay or by being consumed by fire.

One's first experience after passing through the gate of death is to
behold a panorama of one's entire life, for all of one's memories are
in the etheric body just released from the physical body. The panorama usually lasts for three or three and a half days, the time it takes
for the etheric body to separate completely from the physical body.
(It can also be stated as the maximum length of time one could have
remained awake while in the physical body.) During the three
days, all these vivid pictures of the earthlife are presented before
one as if spread out in space. Richard Wagner was right when he
said, "Time becomes space." The whole life, thus spread out, is
reviewed in a mighty tableau. This memory tableau is often experienced by persons who have nearly drowned, fallen from a height,
or been in an accident. The sudden precipitation of falling, the near
drowning, or sudden shock loosens the etheric body to the extent
that one sees the life-panorama; but the etheric is not entirely detached, therefore death does not ensue. Then, when the etheric
forces are restored to the physical body, memory of seeing the
life-review remains.

In the three-day period after death, while the panoramic review
is taking place, there should be no disturbance and no embalming.
(Alternatives, as already mentioned, are dry ice or a sealed casket.)
There should be quietude, preferably a peaceful spiritual mood, so
that the memory tableau can be experienced in tranquillity, without interruption. Cremation should not take place until the end of
the three days, or better, three and a half days. In respect to cremation, Rudolf Steiner suggested it be a matter of personal preference,
with two exceptions. Cremation is inimical for suicides and for
utter materialists. The suicide's time for normal death had not yet
come. It was not time for the etheric body to be released, hence it
remains too closely connected with the physical and cannot so
readily separate from it. Also, in the case of a hardened materialist,
the etheric forces are too deeply bound with the physical to be
detached properly at the time of death.

After the three-day tableau, the etheric body separates from the astral body and ego, and is absorbed into the etheric world. According to its quality, it either impoverishes the higher world or provides nourishment for higher Beings who expect fruit from the earthlife. As the etheric body expands in the universe of ether, it becomes a background, a sort of "firmament," in which one sees what one contributed to the cosmos of ether; something harmful insofar as one was selfish and had no spiritual interests, or beneficial if one had expressed goodwill and been devoted to the spirit.

There is an interesting fact about the withdrawal of the etheric body that may be helpful to you; also, through knowing it, you may be able to help others. The etheric forces of persons who have a close relationship are so interwoven that when the etheric body of one departs at the moment of death, it leaves a condition comparable to rents or holes in the etheric body of the person who remains on earth. That is what produces the great sense of loneliness, pain, and grief that lasts until these rents are healed. Unless something occurs from the spiritual side, it often takes as long as three years, and sometimes even five years, for the etheric restoration to occur, enabling one to adjust to separation from the loved one.

I can speak from firsthand experience. After my husband passed through the gate of death, the first few days were really difficult despite all I knew about life after death. It seemed that my life would be empty without him. Then at the funeral my etheric body was completely healed. The funeral was a magnificent spiritual experience. When I awakened during the following night, I was overwhelmed with joy at the realization that the world is filled with spirit and every human being is a spiritual being. There was no trace of emptiness, for the etheric body had been healed and filled. Then I would write,

> Enriched is all I see
> Because I walked with thee.

A woman who attended my husband John's funeral told her husband when she returned home that she had just been in heaven. He said, "I thought that you went to a funeral." She replied, "Yes, I did, but it was heaven. I wondered if we dared experience such joy." This experience was shared by the people present. This gives an indication of what is possible, what can be, if there is spiritual insight and if spiritual Beings intervene.

That does not often happen in this age of materialism. I was extremely grateful to John because I knew he made it possible. Also, the fact that the ritual of the Christian Community lent itself to such an experience, and the further fact that at the funeral were so many friends who brought their love, making this a happy send-off, like a farewell for someone who is going away and is given a joyous departure. Thus, the soul is not burdened or held back.

Think of what people do when human beings die. It is tragic what sometimes happens. Of course, the mourners are uninformed and unaware, hence one should not criticize them. Nevertheless, because of their ignorance much harm is done to themselves, to the deceased, and to the cosmos. And often much expense is entailed. Sometimes families spend most of their savings, thinking that is going to help the departed loved one, whereas it is the soul and spirit that should be of primary concern. To spiritual vision, physical death becomes transformed into spiritual birth. The soul and spirit are released from the confinement of earthlife into the expanses of world-existence.

The funeral service for the young should be different from that for the elderly. The young are still close to the spiritual worlds; it is the parents who need the greater help. Old persons, however, require the type of service that will rightly release them from the earth and make their homecoming to higher worlds beautiful through the aid of the Angels and the guidance of the Christ.

Rudolf Steiner's vision of supersensible events led him to say that the time will come when people will realize that funerals are more important than meetings of parliaments or congresses. Significant impulses are brought into human affairs on earth if the right connection is made with souls who have passed through the gate of death. They help us tremendously, far more than we realize, when we have decisions to make; and in many experiences of life we receive counsel, help, and advice from them, even if we may not be directly aware of its source.

Loved ones on earth often say, "I cannot believe there is life after death, for if there were, my beloved would have communicated with me in some way." The physical body is the instrument for communication during earthly life. The person who passes through the gate of death lays aside the physical instrument and lives on only as soul and spirit (A). Thenceforth, no communication is possible except on the soul and spirit level, and that is precluded for the person still in the body, if his consciousness erected a "wall" between body and soul (B). Therefore, there is little wonder that there can be no communication. On the other hand, if a person has dissolved the wall, then he functions consciously as soul and spirit in the earthly body and there can be a sense of relationship (C).

spirit	spirit	spirit
soul	soul	soul
~~body~~	body	body
A	B	C

Three possible relationships between soul, spirit, and the physical body

Sometimes the very experience of the departure of a loved one helps to dissolve the wall, or gives a momentary breakthrough. In the moment of grief or desperation, in that moment of sorrow, sometimes a light dawns. In general, however, for the average person in our materialistic age, there is no conscious connection. One of the fruits of spiritual science is that the wall gradually dissolves, and souls on earth and those in the supersensible spheres can be of far greater mutual help to each other.

A giant step is taken when grief is changed to gratitude. An experience at an earthly airport departure gate will illustrate the application of this principle. The night before our separation after two joyous weeks together—our first meeting in nearly forty years—a very dear friend said, "I'm afraid I'll cry when you leave." I replied, "Oh no. We shall not think about parting. We shall have only joy because we'll be filled with gratitude that we could have this time together." And so it was.

To mourn because we no longer have our "departed" loved ones with us in the flesh is an ungrateful feeling. And to have the feeling that we have lost them weighs them down. We should rather be thankful we did have them with us, and be grateful that they enriched our lives. By the upwelling of gratitude and by outstreaming love we create an atmosphere that selflessly connects us with them. There is rejoicing when we change our attitude from grief to gratitude.

When a friend of mine was notified that her husband in the hospital was near death, she called a priest of the Christian Community who went with her at once to the hospital. While the priest was giving the last anointing, the man passed through the gate of death. It was a beautiful departure, although he had not previously been concerned with spiritual things. He had not been antagonistic, but his daily affairs took up his time and he postponed giving his attention to spiritual realities. His wife, who for years had been devoted to Anthroposophy, said that at the moment he passed through the gate of death she felt, "I haven't lost him; we will always be together." Her first feeling was a sense of closer relationship.

At the funeral a few days later, the Christian Community ritual was followed by a warm tribute from a close business associate. It seemed to be a meaningful experience for the one who had died, and the priest said to me, "I am sure he was present here and experienced all that took place." After some days my friend telephoned me and said, "I feel a weight on my chest, as though he wants something. I don't know what it is." I told her that very likely he wanted information that he had not sought during his earthly life, that is, knowledge of higher worlds. I mentioned that Rudolf Steiner often recommended reading to the dead, and suggested she take something that is meaningful from spiritual science, especially that which relates to the soul world and spirit world, and man's experiences in those worlds, also the cycle of lectures entitled "The Gospel of St. John." She started reading to him, whereupon the sense of heaviness and of his wanting something left her.

Rudolf Steiner, who with supersensible sight could follow souls beyond death, observed that often when people during their earth-life repudiate this knowledge and even vigorously reject it, in the depths of their souls they are crying out for it, longing for it. Then, after death, when they are free from the body that blinded them and brought the objection, the soul expresses its true desire and tries to obtain illumination from some loved one or interested person on earth who has the light.

Those who have passed over the threshold of death, and who long for light, can be benefited also when groups meet to study the science of the spirit, for it is a language they can understand concerning the soul and spirit, and the spheres in which they dwell. In regard to reading to souls in the supersensible world, keep in mind that one should invite them, and that one should think clearly what one is reading, either silently or aloud, without interrupting continuity. If one's mind wanders, or one thinks of something else and then continues reading, it is to them as it would be to us if, while we were reading, the print would suddenly disappear, and then reappear again. If we concentrate on what we read and if we think the thought clearly, the departed can comprehend it, and it illumines the soul world for them.

Most people do not want to face the experience of their own death. They say, "I'll wait and see. It is time enough when I get to the other side to find out what will happen." Such a wait-and-see attitude would be unthinkable if one were to take a journey on earth. One seeks to learn as much as possible about one's destination. The most important journey we shall ever take deserves even greater—the greatest—consideration and foreknowledge. And more so, since our orientation and our experiences in the planetary spheres are conditioned by our every thought, word, feeling, and deed during our sojourn on earth.

In the light of investigations of near-death experiences, something new needs to be added to what was written years ago. The wait-and-see attitude prevalent today is the result of materialism which tore asunder the microcosm and the macrocosm, the subjective and the objective within human consciousness. The awareness was lost that what occurs in the subjective human soul produces effects in the objective cosmos. For example, a lie darkens the astral light in the macrocosm, and a loveless action is destructive in the cosmos. What human beings regard as their inmost thoughts and feelings are actually connected with objective cosmic development.

Human and cosmic evolution are interwoven, and they metamorphose together. The diagram on page 76 shows that in the twentieth century a new spiritual stream appeared, introducing a spiritual world-conception. This subjective change, relating the microcosm once more with the macrocosm, parallels an objective change, a new Christ-event. As the time was ripe nearly 2,000 years ago for the Christ to appear in *physical* form, so now, in the twentieth century, and particularly since the 1930s, the time has come for the Christ to manifest in *etheric* form. This is the awaited "second coming" which, however, will *never* be in physical form. Increasingly is his very real presence experienced, also, during earthlife, especially in times of dire need.

Moreover, the time has come, as foreseen by Rudolf Steiner in spiritual vision and announced in October 1911, that in the second half of the twentieth century the Christ would become the Lord of Destiny (Karma).[1] The Christ has taken over the function, formerly ascribed to Moses or to St. Peter, as the accountant of destiny, meeting one at the gate of death when the etheric body separates from the physical body and the panoramic review objectifies all one's memories. The Christ is then present as a Being of indescribable light, emanating love and kindness while He asks what one has done with one's life.[2]

Beginning in our era, the Etheric Christ meets every soul at the gate of death and receives an account of its destiny, including all the good deeds as well as the foolish and evil ones. As the Lord of Destiny, he will bring order into one's destiny in such a way that in the future incarnations the destiny will be worked out not only to accord with individual requirements, but in a manner that will best serve the entire human race, and thus promote the progress of humanity as a whole.

With the giving over of the etheric body to the cosmic ethers following the life-review, the astral body and ego are free to enter the Moon sphere for purification of the astral body before one can journey to higher planetary spheres.

17

THE INNER PLANETARY SPHERES—
THE MOON, MERCURY, AND VENUS

IF THE Universe were merely the vast machine described by astrophysicists, the journey through the cosmos which we shall describe would be impossible. Spiritual science, however, reveals that the heavenly bodies are the signposts to us of colonies of spiritual Beings of varied ranks, each with appointed tasks, the performing of which collectively makes possible the grand maintenance of our Father's house and the evolution of the universe, earth, and man.

After passing through the gate of death and experiencing the memory-tableau, our cosmic journey takes us first through the inner planetary spheres—the Moon, Mercury, and Venus—then the Sun sphere, followed by the outer planetary spheres—Mars, Jupiter, and Saturn—on to the zodiac, and back, in reverse order, to the earth. We shall describe these spheres one by one, keeping in mind that *by "sphere" we mean not merely the planetary body we see illuminated in the sky, but the sphere formed by using the distance from the earth to the planet as the radius.* In this sense, we are in all the spheres all the time we live on earth, and we are influenced by them whether we are conscious of them or not. After passing through the gate of death our consciousness expands outward from the earth into these spheres. Although the supersensible is beyond space, it reflects into space, and the planets can rightly be used as markers to represent spiritual regions.

The first sphere we enter is *the Moon sphere,* which comprises everything within the orbit of the Moon. Some souls with deep earthly attachments remain near the earth for a time, or may even be earth-bound. Usually there is a gradual "expansion" away from the earth, yet while we are in the Moon sphere we remain earth-centered. The Moon as the satellite of the earth is itself earth-centered.

In the Moon sphere we have to cleanse ourselves from and cast off everything that attached us to purely earthly sense-perception.

Purgatory is an appropriate word because it means purging, cleansing, cleaning. Try to recall everything you did today, or yesterday, that did not relate to sense-impressions. How much is left? Probably not much. Thus you begin to realize how little of our activity is related to what is beyond the sense-perceptible.

It is obvious that we cannot take the physical body into the soul world. No more can we take the soul into the spiritual world. The soul must first have cleansed itself from everything that attached it to the earth before the spirit can free itself from the soul and expand into the outer planetary spheres. Everything in the soul that related us to the earth in a personal way has to be purged and transformed before we can journey on further and enter the spiritual world, or even the higher realms of the soul world.

The purging process should not be regarded as punishment, but as a necessity of the soul world. Just as a ship is not adapted for land travel, nor an automobile for sea voyages, so the earthly inclined soul is not adapted for journeying through higher planetary spheres. In conformity with the laws of the soul world, the soul itself demands its purification.

Judging with our earthly conceptions we are apt to consider the experiences in the Moon sphere as dreadful, but not so in the soul world where they are known to be a blessing inasmuch as they perfect the soul and prepare it for the larger, higher mansions of our Father's house. It would be exceedingly presumptious to expect to abide in our Father's house with our souls soiled with self-seeking and unsatisfied earthly desires.

It is a cosmic necessity to be first cleansed, and to face our true worth for the cosmos, before we can proceed beyond the Moon sphere. As a child after birth only gradually learns to use the physical body and adjust itself to the physical world, so after death the soul-spirit must adjust to the soul world.

The lowest realm of the soul world is the region of burning desire. On entering this realm the soul has all the desires it had in earthlife. When we give up the body, the soul has not altered an iota at the outset. We take with us all the desires and attitudes we had on the earth. A great craving for food or for a cigarette cannot be satisfied since we are without a body, yet the desire is still there. We have to cleanse ourselves from all the burning desires that require earthly and bodily conditions for their satisfaction. Persons who have made sincere efforts to cleanse themselves on the earth, persons who have not detached themselves from earthlife but are not held by it, can by-pass or very quickly emerge from this lowest realm. They have already cleansed and purified their souls and filled themselves with spiritual light.

The essential fact is that in the Moon sphere we have to wean ourselves from all earthly connections and conditions. In addition to our sense-impressions, already mentioned, all thoughts that relate only to things of the outer world have to be eliminated. Also, all the wishes of our heart have to be cleansed. Everything in this realm is personal, concerning ourselves alone. Finally, after purging our souls from our burning desires, our thoughts and wishes that related us to the earth, there may remain a hankering for the earthlife as a whole. From this, too, we must at last detach ourselves. It is not a comfortable experience for souls unless on earth they experienced something beyond the purely personal, physical, and material.

In the Moon sphere all of our life's experiences are gone over from the last of life to the first. What actually happens is that we go through our sleep-life from the last night backwards to the beginning of earthlife, for every night in sleep the preceding day's experiences are reviewed and are recorded by the Moon Beings; hence in the backward flow of the periods of sleep, we experience the record of our entire day-life. Inasmuch as sleep constitutes approximately one-third of our earthly life, the length of this review is equivalent to about a third of the span of our years on earth.

What we experienced during earthlife unconsciously in sleep is relived after death in an awareness much more intense than waking life, just as the waking life is clearer than dreaming. This is made possible by the Moon Beings who now pronounce stern judgment upon all our good and evil. It is a cosmic verdict evaluating the worth or harm to the universe of our good and evil. We become vividly aware of what the spiritual Beings think about the deeds, feelings, and thoughts of our earthlife. The angels are the guardians of our individual destiny; the archangels evaluate our deeds in connection with the nation and the language that were ours. The archai assess the value our deeds had for the epoch of time we lived on earth.

If we did wrong and brought harm to the cosmos, or even did what was worthless for the cosmos, we feel enveloped in cold and in darkness, which seem to rob us of our very existence and extinguish our consciousness. If, on the other hand, we did what was valuable to the cosmos, we feel bathed in light and warmth which fill us with fresh life and increased consciousness.

A significant fact about this process of evaluation is that if we made someone unhappy, or caused him great distress, or injured him, we do not feel the indifference about it, or perhaps even the elation we felt on earth when we committed the deed. We do not experience the anger or satisfaction that we felt, but rather what other persons felt as a result of our thoughts, feelings, and deeds. We actually feel what others experienced. All the pain and suffering we inflicted on others we now feel as they felt it. We experience the effect on others of all that we did or failed to do. Suicides, especially, suffer the intense grief they caused others.

Meanwhile, after having laid aside the physical and etheric bodies on passing through the gate of death, we have become beings of moral value, expressions of our own spiritual significance, and we have assumed a spirit-form. Although this spirit-form resembles the physical form, it is wholly supersensible and in constant transformation. It can in reality be called a moral physiognomy, for it reveals our moral value. For example, the chest region of the spirit-form shows whether we were cowardly or courageous. The arms and hands are especially expressive of the moral nature, whereas the head becomes less so and gradually disappears. The entire spirit-form is a physiognomy revealing our moral qualities. What in earthly life we thought was hidden becomes completely revealed in the spirit-form. We appear as we truly are in our soul nature. There can be no pretense. There is no hiding anything. Indeed, "There is nothing covered, that shall not be revealed; neither hid, that shall not be known" (Luke 12:2).

In the inner planetary spheres we meet only those with whom we have been connected by ties of destiny. It is the link of destiny that gives us the power to "see" the moral physiognomies of others. It is no seeing with physical eyes, but a kind of feeling perception which gives a close, intimate, mutual scrutiny. At first, however, we perceive only those who are like ourselves. Like can only distinguish like. We know that angels, too, are present in the Moon sphere, but we cannot relate to them unless in our physiognomical spirit-form we come to resemble them. We must fashion ourselves to resemble what we wish to perceive and this requires will.

How do we progress and rise out of the Moon sphere? Here it is mainly *will* that counts. We finally realize, "If I will to do it, I can move on; I can overcome the conditions. I can will to outgrow the earthly and the personal, will to purify my selfish desires, will to be more like the angels." When we achieve this, we can progress to higher spheres. Our evil, however, has been registered and must be left behind in the Moon sphere, where we shall have to confront it again on returning to this sphere before rebirth on the earth.

During earthly life we are in all of the planetary spheres all the time, for the spheres interpenetrate. We are apt to think of the spiritual worlds too much in spatial terms, yet the various planetary spheres, the mansions of our Father's house, represent in a sense an expansion, and certainly an *expansion of consciousness*. An initiate on the earth can be conscious in every sphere. It is a matter of consciousness, of tuning in. We are in all the spheres, but awareness depends on heightened consciousness. After death, having accomplished the cleansing, the evaluating, and the necessary willed transformation in the Moon sphere, we can go on to the Mercury and Venus spheres.

From the spiritual viewpoint, the sequence of the spheres of the inner planets, those between the earth and the Sun, is given as Moon, Mercury, and Venus. This follows the time cycles of their sidereal revolutions—Moon 28 days, Mercury 88 days, and Venus 225 days—that is, the relationship of time rather than of space. The spiritual sequence will here be adhered to, as also will the characteristics Rudolf Steiner ascribed to them in his later years, 1917–1924.

Again, it should be noted that there are no rigid lines of demarcation between the spheres; they are not fixed as are our earthly boundaries. The inner planetary spheres are especially flexible and mobile because our experiences there are personal and subjective, connected with our past earthlife; and the earthlives of no two persons are exactly the same. Recall the illustration of the matching hands. Passage through the inner spheres is as variable as the lives of individuals; therefore, only certain generalizations can be given.

The forces of the inner planetary spheres are centripetal, working inward, or backward, to our earthlife. We cannot advance to the Sun sphere and beyond it before our last earthlife has been worked over and we have released ourselves from everything that related us to the earth. The earth has to fade away before we can experience the outer planetary spheres.

The Moon sphere is totally connected with the past, whereas in the Mercury and Venus spheres we realize how what we did on earth has to be changed for our future life. We see how recompense can be made. We see how we shall have to change things in order to work them out in our future destiny.

A characteristic of these three spheres is that we cannot change the past; we cannot alter any shortcomings. If we realize that we have not had sufficient love, we cannot increase that love now. Nothing can be done to change the past. What we *can* do is to resolve to correct it for the next life. That is how the future now enters into our experiences. If we see wherein we failed, or what we lack, we cannot fill in the lack, but we can prepare to make amends in the next earthly life. What we bind on earth is bound in heaven.

Homer was aware of this truth when he stated, "We enter the world in which there is no change." Not that we do not change from one sphere to another, but we cannot change what we had made of ourselves on earth. Steiner uses this illustration: It is as though you wanted to move and you found yourself chained to the ground. You may have had dreams of that nature in which you wanted so desperately to get somewhere and you found that you were somehow held back and could not move forward. It is somewhat like that in the soul world. We realize our mistakes and we cannot change them except as we resolve to be different in the succeeding earthly life. We need to realize our shortcomings in order to prepare the astral body rightly for the future. Our moral blemishes, our personal imperfections, must be left in the Moon sphere.

In the next region, the Mercury sphere, we are freed from the spiritual consequences of illness. Mercury is the guardian of the secrets of illness and health and in past ages has rightly been associated with authentic wisdom about healing and medicine. The caduceus, the staff of Mercury, is the emblem of the medical profession.

Healing, however, relates to the soul as well as to the body. In the Mercury sphere it befalls souls who lacked conscience and did not adhere to truth to be compelled for a time to be servants of those beings who bring about disease, accidents, and premature death. There are actual beings who bring about accidents, and we become their servants if on earth we were liars and were without conscience. On the other hand, if we worked with enthusiasm, if we performed tasks and did things not only out of a sense of duty but with real love and enthusiasm, then we help those powers that bring health and well-being to mankind on earth. Beneficial forces then flow from the Mercury realm to the earth.

If on the earth we were indolent, lazy, or lovers of ease, we are compelled for a time to be servants of the beings who have to bring about obstacles and hindrances in the physical world. It is indeed a moral world-order in which we live, even if people know it not. It is the "wall" that has obscured the moral world and blocked out all thought of a moral order. People think that they get by with things in the physical world, not knowing that in the higher worlds they will be held accountable for every thought, feeling, and action or inaction.

In earthlife we may have had intentions which we never carried to completion. These are inscribed in the Moon sphere. Such intentions concerned only one's personal life. If other persons were involved, as, for example, a promise we did not fulfill, then we reap the consequences in the Mercury sphere where such records are preserved. For example, a business man who repeatedly made vain promises told me that everyone lies now and that the days of the golden rule are past.

In our spirit-form, revealing our moral physiognomy, we experience a connection only with those whom we had some earthly tie. We see each other exactly as we are, for our spirit-form openly portrays our true moral nature. In the Moon sphere it is still blank perception, a mere beholding. In the Mercury sphere we advance to an understanding of what we had been beholding. We come to know what people really thought of us. There is revealed what it is in the physiognomy which points back to the common destiny, and we see in perspective how our future lives will have to take a certain course to work out our destiny.

There should also unfold an understanding for the spiritual Beings with whom we mingle. However, if human souls were materialists on earth, if they rejected everything of a supersensible nature, they will have little understanding of the angels, archangels, and archai who comprise the Third Hierarchy. They rank above us, just as animals, plants, and minerals rank below man on the earth. How we relate to these spiritual companions in the soul realm depends on our religious attitudes on earth.

Terrible isolation, far more intense than any earthly loneliness, is felt in the Mercury sphere by souls who on earth had no belief in supersensible realities. Because of their blindness to the spirit, they suffer a hermit-like existence even when in the midst of spiritual Beings. They cannot now understand what on earth they had rejected. Hence, the wait-and-see attitude toward death can lead to unpleasant and even disastrous results. It is important to remember that by our conduct on earth we condition our experiences in the soul world. We condition ourselves for loneliness or association, for sorrow or joy.

In the Venus sphere we meet angels, archangels, and archai who have attained a higher stage of development than those in the Mercury sphere. Here, likewise, we have no understanding of these Beings if on earth we were rank materialists. Whether or not we feel alien or at home in the Venus realm depends on our capacity of *love*. If we radiated love on earth, we here feel our souls flooded with cosmic love. On the other hand, if we harbored hatred, even unconsciously, then the cosmic love forces are metamorphosed and arise in us as forces of wrath and fury. To subdue the wrath and to harmonize one's soul with the cosmos requires *will*.

Our passage through the Mercury and Venus spheres depends on our relationship to the higher Beings and to one another. These two qualities are encompassed in the dual commandment: "Thou shalt love the Lord thy God with all thy heart, and with all thy soul, and with all thy strength, and with all thy mind; and thy neighbor as thyself" (Luke 10:27).

It was necessary first to have had our personal experiences of the past earthly life assessed in the inner planetary spheres and there to "check our moral bundle" before journeying, as beings of spirit, further into the cosmos, into the glorious sphere of the Sun.

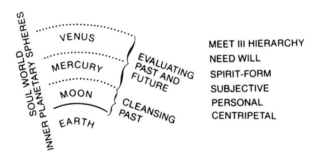

The soul's passage from earth into the soul
world, the inner planetary spheres

18

THE SUN SPHERE

ONE characteristic of life is its constant metamorphosis. Thinking that is alive cannot conceive of eternal life as mere continuance without change. The changes from birth to death are obvious. And although the metamorphoses from death to a new birth are visible only to the spiritual seer, they are comprehensible to those who have not yet developed the power to see for themselves. Thus far we have traced the changes the human being undergoes after passing through the gate of death and journeying through the soul world. On completing the experiences in the soul world, the spirit is released from the fetters of the soul, and with a feeling of bliss at the emancipation it enters the Sun sphere.

As the Sun is the center and heart of our solar system, so the spiritual-Sun existence is the central realm through which we journey outward into the wide reaches of the cosmos. We stay in the Sun sphere much longer than in the other spheres. To insure that there is no misunderstanding, it should be emphasized that by the Sun sphere we do not mean the shining globe of gas we behold from the earth. To spiritual vision the Sun is a colony of spiritual Beings whose radiations extend throughout the cosmos. So vast and varied are our experiences in this central realm, leading from the soul world of the inner planetary spheres—Moon, Mercury, Venus—to the spirit world of the outer spheres—Mars, Jupiter, Saturn—that only a few aspects can be presented here.

In the inner spheres everything was personal and related back to the earth, or was concerned with how in the future we should change what we were. There we had a spirit-form, our souls were cleansed, and our earthlife was evaluated and judged by the Beings of the Third Hierarchy, the angels, archangels, and archai. Whatever was evil had to be left behind before entering the majestic Sun sphere, which is a moral realm of pure, radiant goodness.

In the inner spheres we related only to those human souls with whom we had a destiny tie and a connection on earth. As we gradually approach the spiritual Sun existence, we enter upon the realm that is universal, a quality reflected in the observable spatial universe. The Moon travels only around the earth. Mercury and Venus orbit the Sun between the earth and the Sun, but the Sun forces ray out into the whole solar system. In the Sun sphere we are brought into connection with *all* mankind, not only with those with whom we were connected by destiny. The heart of our solar system embraces all humanity.

To the degree that we meet certain qualifications, we are able to experience the spiritual Sun existence more consciously, more fully and freely. The preparation to meet these qualifications had to be made during earthlife; therefore, this knowledge of the cosmos is not something remote, but exceedingly practical. One quality we need is a true sense of our own ego. As we need sense organs in the physical world, so we need our "I" in the sphere of the Sun. The Sun environment speaks through our ego, just as colors, sounds, warmth, etc., in our earthly environment are perceived by our physical sense organs. Lacking any of the sense organs, our experience of the outer world is incomplete; we are handicapped in establishing a full, wholesome relation with the physical world.

Inasmuch, then, as one's ego is comparable to a sense organ in the Sun sphere, we should be aware of the importance of the right development of the "I." We should not be weak beings with little or no self-consciousness. Today, ego consciousness is endangered by drugs and by all forms of supression of individual freedom, whether by the state (e.g., communism), by groups (e.g., unions), or by any kind of dictatorship, even in the home. Nor should we be egotists. We should have a true sense of egohood and our worth as individuals.

And more than this, we should have had on earth a friendly relationship with *all* other egos without any exclusion, a comprehension of what is common to all humanity, and an understanding of and tolerance for all religious beliefs. As the Sun shines upon all mankind, on the evil and the good alike, in our earthlife we should have been outgoing without any prejudice. In the Sun sphere the emphasis is on the universal human and on *feeling*, instead of on will as in the inner planetary spheres. Here in the sphere of the Sun, the heart of our solar system, the heart plays a large part. The saying of St. Paul that in Christ "there is neither Jew nor Greek, there is neither bond nor free," we might paraphrase today, "In Christ there is neither white nor black, neither laborer nor executive director." The universal human is what counts. All-embracing love fostered on earth enables us to find our way to other egos in the Sun sphere.

An important qualification needed for the sun realm—in addition to a strong ego consciousness of the right kind, and a feeling of kinship with all human beings—is a relationship to the Christ and insight into the Christ Mystery. Not even initiates are able to find the Christ in the Sun sphere if they have not related to him on earth. Consider the difference between B.C. and A.D. times. In the ages before Christ men were still given religious teachings that enabled them to meet the Christ in the Sun sphere after death, for that is where the Christ was. However since the Mystery of Golgotha, Christ is in the earth sphere and is "the Lord of the heavenly forces upon Earth." Now we find him in the Sun realm only if we have found him on the earth. As stated, this was not true in B.C. times. Conditions have changed. In our time we can find the Christ, who is the Sublime Sun Being, only if we have related to him in freedom during earthlife.

In the realm of the spiritual Sun, we meet the Second Hierarchy, the Beings called Spirits of Form (or Elohim), the Spirits of Movement, and the Spirits of Wisdom. Their names in Greek, used in esoteric Christianity, are Exusiai, Dynamis, and Kyriotetes. These exalted Beings are higher and more advanced than the Beings of the Third Hierarchy in the inner planetary spheres. Our relationship to them depends on our good intentions, our moral goodness manifested on earth. In physical existence on earth there often appears to be little justice; the good are sometimes unfortunate, whereas the bad appear to succeed. In the Sun sphere it is our intention that counts.

Modern science gives validity to natural laws, but not to moral laws, and now millions of people deny the existence of a moral world order. In the spiritual Sun existence it is otherwise. The Sun sphere is the province of these purely spiritual Beings of the Second Hierarchy, whose moral world we behold as directly as we do the kingdoms of nature on the earth. No activities related to nature are to be found in the sphere of the Sun, only moral activities, the effects of goodness. It is a purely moral world. Evil thoughts, though left behind in the Moon sphere, isolate us from the Beings of the Second Hierarchy. Good thoughts, and even good intentions, enable us to understand the language of the Sun Beings and to mingle with them.

Here morality is a reality; and instead of the cleansing and evaluating experiences of the inner spheres, there is sublime activity
in the Sun sphere in cooperation with other human beings and with
the Beings of the Second Hierarchy. With these Beings we are
co-builders of the cosmos. People sometimes speak of souls going,
after death, to their "eternal rest," and they think of heaven as a
place of bliss and rest. What a misconception! It is a realm not of
rest but of tremendous, sublime activity in which the spirit-form—
which in the inner planetary spheres was a physiognomical form
revealing the qualities of our character—is gradually transformed
into a sun-like spirit-sphere. It is "rounded off," becomes spherical,
and reflects the whole universe.

In the early stages of our cosmic journey, the spiritual forces of
the head gradually dissolved in a spiritual mist; now the spiritual
forces of the rest of the spirit-form are metamorphosed into a sphere
that will become the spirit-germ for the head in the next earthlife.
The spiritual forces of the legs are transformed into the forces for
the lower jaw in the next life, and the forces of the arms, into those
of the upper jaw. Keep in mind that the head itself portrays the
threefoldness of one's entire organism: the rounded skull and brain
correlate with the head proper; the nose with the rhythmic system;
and the mouth and jaws with the metabolic-limb system. Recall that
the head formation predominates in the embryo, and that in the
spiritually conceived Sistine Madonna, Raphael surrounded the
Madonna and Child with clouds of heads.

Describing the awe-inspiring spiritual process of transforming
man's lower being into the upper being for the next earthlife,
Rudolf Steiner said, "in comparison with it, any work that is done
on earth in whatsoever domain is utterly insignificant. Great and
majestic is the work that is accomplished by man in the spiritual
world in union with higher spiritual Beings! There, in the sphere of
the Sun (using the word in its wider sense) the secret of man's
being is worked out."[1] Human beings also take part in the infinite
grandeur of the process of metamorphosis, and by working together
they form spiritual kinships which bring them together intimately
in earthlife.

The newly formed spirit-sphere, shaped in the likeness of the
Sun, reflects what we now experience in the Sun sphere as the
"Music of the Spheres." Our spirit-sphere is itself sound, express-
ing in cosmic tone our true nature. The music of the spheres is more

than a poetic phrase; it is a reality in the Sun sphere. Into this music there rise certain dissonances that come from the degeneration of earthly language and of the true meaning of the word, revealed in much of the poor articulation and the jargon used nowadays. This corruption rises as far as the Sun sphere and might be compared with radio static that causes interference and discord. On the other hand, we are filled through and through with a universal feeling as we experience the cosmic harmonies and melodies born from the interworking of the starry worlds and the different orders of Beings of the cosmos. This glorious music of the spheres accompanies us as we journey further.

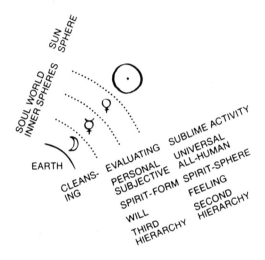

The spirit's experience in the Sun sphere

In contemplating the experiences we have in the Sun sphere, we begin to realize what a wonderful cosmic creation man is, and that the spiritual Sun is where future generations of human beings are initially prepared for their next earthlives. As we journey through all the planetary spheres, we never lose an awareness of our connection with the earth, else the earth would become foreign to us at the next incarnation. But this connection with the earth is more intense in the Sun sphere. It is then that we view the earth from the Sun. As the healthy soul on earth takes for granted a supersensible world beyond the material world, so in the Sun sphere between death and rebirth we regard the earth as the world "beyond." It is an intense experience, not so much in relation to one's own destiny, but an appreciation of the intrinsic character of earth existence as a whole. From the Sun sphere, our journey leads into the outer planetary spheres of Mars, Jupiter, and Saturn, where the wonderful creative activity continues.

19

THE OUTER PLANETARY SPHERES—
MARS, JUPITER, SATURN—
AND THE ZODIAC

IN ANCIENT times before man became so deeply immersed in the physical body, he knew himself to be a being of soul and spirit related to the spirituality of the cosmos, a cosmos more real to him than was the physical world. He remembered his life in the spiritual world before coming to birth. And death did not then have the finality it has for modern man, for death did not set nothingness in the place of life. Beyond death ancient man perceived worlds of exalted spiritual Beings and their deeds.

These worlds and Beings are still there, but we have lost the spiritual vision with which to perceive them today. Now is the time when the perceptive faculties, which were instinctive and dreamlike in ancient man, should be regained on a fully self-conscious level by modern man. A pioneer in this new consciousness was the "scientific seer," Rudolf Steiner. In spite of language being limited to the physical and earthly world, he described in understandable terms and from varied viewpoints the vast riches of the supersensible realms, Beings, and events.

Even during earthlife, we, as beings of body, soul, and spirit, are linked with those supersensible realms, and after we pass through the gate of death, which frees us from the physical form, we journey through those regions. First, as soul and spirit in the inner planetary spheres of the Moon, Mercury, and Venus, we confront the after-effects of the last earthlife and we complete the cleansing of the soul and evaluation of our earthly experiences. Then, free from the subjective soul qualities, we can advance to the central region, the Sun sphere where, amid the music of the spheres and the sublime activity of transforming the spirit-form into a spirit-sphere in cooperation with the exalted Sun Beings, we experience the universal human.

Only then are we able to emerge from the Sun sphere as pure spirit and enter the spirit world of the outer planetary spheres,

Mars, Jupiter, Saturn, and of the zodiac, and the vast cosmic ocean of the world of the stars. In all these realms tremendous tasks relating to the cosmos await us. However, our earthlife determines not only the nature of our personal, subjective experiences in the inner planetary spheres, but also the degree of *consciousness* we can maintain in the Sun sphere and beyond. The importance of this fact cannot be overemphasized. Therefore we need to dwell further on the qualifications required for clear consciousness, inner beatitude, and infinite blessedness in the higher supersensible worlds.

These qualifications have changed in the course of the ages. In the epochs when man still felt connected with the primal sources of all religions he could, on reaching the Sun sphere after death, feel united with all humanity and the lofty Sun Beings, the most majestic of whom was the Christ who illuminated their Sun existence and led them further into the cosmos. As mankind became increasingly estranged from spiritual realities and would ultimately have lost connection with the spirit, the Christ left his sublime Sun realm, came to the earth, and through the Mystery of Golgotha, a supersensible event in the sense world, he united himself with the earth and will remain with it until the end of earth existence.

Henceforth he manifests his majestic glory and guidance to souls in the Sun sphere, and beyond, *only* if they have in freedom related themselves to him on the earth. Until modern times, the soul's relation to Christ was more on the feeling or astral level, whereas now it is necessary to advance to conscious-ego comprehension and to a recognition of the cosmological significance of the Mystery of Golgotha, a spiritual event which was at the same time an event of the physical plane.

Christ is the only divine Being who experienced death, for death is experienced only on the earth. In supersensible realms there are changes of consciousness but not death. To understand the magnitude of Christ's deed it is not enough to respect him as a great teacher; one must in some measure comprehend his death, and this can be comprehended only on earth where death occurs.

If Christ is our guide as we journey through the cosmos between death and rebirth, we more easily recognize our spiritual surroundings, are able to move freely as social beings in the Sun sphere, and to understand all souls irrespective of their beliefs, for Christ passed through the Mystery of Golgotha for all mankind. Moreover, in the Sun sphere we can prepare a strong, vigorous etheric body for our next incarnation. And beyond the Sun, with Christ, we can maintain our ego consciousness; without Christ we would be asleep and lose ourselves in the fulness and vast wealth of wisdom of the cosmos. Then we are able to create freely out of this wisdom, not only to prepare faculties for becoming better human beings in the next earthlife, but also for becoming a better force in the evolution of the earth.

Our expansion into the outer planetary spheres brings us into the realms of the activities of the Beings of the First Hierarchy: the Thrones in the Mars sphere, the Cherubim in the Jupiter sphere, and the Seraphim in the Saturn sphere. In the vision Isaiah had when he received his call (chapter 6), he beheld the Seraphim. To this day, people sing about the Cherubim and Seraphim in the hymn, "Holy, Holy, Holy," written in 1827 by Bishop Reginald Heber, but what do they know about these exalted Beings? Do they believe that they really exist?

How conscious are we of them as we journey through the outer planetary spheres between death and rebirth? What we were and did on earth determines what we experience in these spiritual realms. A comparison sometimes made is that of an animal, such as a dog, being in the presence of human beings who are constructing a building. The dog is there, yet it knows nothing about, and cannot participate in, the construction going on around it. Similarly, we can be in the presence of the Thrones, Cherubim, and Seraphim, yet not know what is happening. We are present but asleep, as it were, in these realms of thought and reason. If we had no spiritual thoughts on earth, and no link with the Christ, our consciousness is dimmed and we pass more quickly through the spiritual world. The more materialistic we were on earth, the more asleep we are in the spiritual world, and the sooner we reincarnate, even while still "unripe" spiritually.

The Mars Sphere

The first sphere beyond the Sun is the Mars sphere. A positive quality of Mars is *courage*. How courageous we were during earthlife is a factor in determining how conscious we are in this realm of cosmic speech. Everything is of a cosmic nature. In the Sun sphere we experienced the music of the spheres, and these pure cosmic harmonies continue into the outer planetary regions. Our entry from the Sun sphere into the Mars realm of *cosmic speech* might be compared with Beethoven's Ninth Symphony in which the music bursts into song; words are added to the music.

In the Mars sphere the cosmic music continues, but mingled with it is cosmic speech. At first we only hear it, then we feel ourselves interwoven in it. We become a part of the symphony of the cosmic word. This is no fleeting word. We speak forth our very being, and reveal ourselves to each other. This speech is infinitely expressive and creative. We no longer are only a spirit-sphere, for in the outer planetary spheres we weave the germ, cosmic in dimension, which will eventually be the spirit-germ for our head in the next earthlife.

The inhabitants of the Mars sphere who are most important for us are the Beings of the First Hierarchy, the knowers of the cosmic word and guardians of the cosmic speech. In addition to them and excarnate human beings, there are among the Mars population war-like beings with no ego or "I" to control the astral body. However, in the great cosmic process of evolution and world-becoming, planets and their populations change. About 400 years ago, at the turn of the sixteenth and seventeenth centuries, there occurred an event of immense importance, which served as a counterbalance to the materialistic age then approaching.[1]

At that time the Mars sphere was permeated and transformed by Gautama Buddha, who thus became the redeemer for Mars, in a similar but lesser way to the Christ becoming the Redeemer for our earth. Through this sacrifice, the peace, compassion, humility, and spiritual quality of Buddha flowed forth to temper and replace the destructive, warlike, militant, aggressive, strife-breeding, conten-tious forces which Mars previously manifested, as well as the con-structive forces of courage, bravery, enthusiasm, energy, and capac-ity for action. As noted, human beings maintain little wakeful consciousness in the Mars sphere unless on earth they have had courage.

As a result of Buddha's mission on Mars, excarnate human beings now passing through this sphere between death and a new birth receive different forces than formerly. Enough time has elapsed since the Buddha performed his peace mission on Mars that some souls who incarnated on earth in recent decades may have been among those who were admonished on passing through the Mars sphere to be less warlike and to promote peace on earth. In the future many more people will reincarnate with less warlike tenden-cies, and with an interest in maintaining an active life of the soul even when engaged in material life. Without withdrawing from external materialistic life, they will be able to manifest a soul life sensitive to the spirit.

Through a comprehension of such interrelationships between the various planets of our solar system, and between the higher Beings with their differentiated missions in carrying forward human evolution, we are impressed anew with the fact that Man is far more than an earthly being; he is in truth a cosmic being, a citizen of the cosmos.

The Jupiter Sphere

From the Mars sphere our journey through the cosmos leads on to the Jupiter sphere where the cosmic word becomes *cosmic thought*. Cosmic thoughts are living realities and are vastly different from our ordinary thoughts. This morning you may have thought about and planned what you would do today or tomorrow, and where you would go. This, of course, is necessary for earthly life, yet it is paltry when compared with cosmic thought and activity. Think what cosmic thought is! It comprises how planets relate to other planets, how worlds evolve, and new ages arise!

On our outward journey the spirit-germ of the head for the next earthlife is first built to understand cosmic speech and cosmic thought. Think what it means to understand the activities of the Beings of the cosmos! Consider all the people who took part in the astronauts' ventures to the Moon, and how they all had to cooperate with one another. Let us try to enlarge our concepts and think of the whole cosmos, of cosmic speech, thought, and activity. The Beings of the Higher Hierarchies not only give life and consciousness to the planets, and keep them moving in their orbits with utmost precision, but they also relate them rightly to each other, maintain the harmony of all of them, and also relate our solar system to other systems.

The qualities that prepare us to be conscious and constructively active in the Jupiter sphere are *reverence,* devotion, and unity with all life. In the Sun sphere the requirement was unity with all human beings, the universal human, but in the Jupiter sphere it is unity with *all* life, and reverence for the unity and harmony of the world.

Our materialistic culture has produced a form of knowledge in which reverence plays no part. Knowledge divorced from reverence threatens to destroy civilization, not only through the invention of destructive weapons but by lowering our image of man to that of a higher animal and disavowing his link to the angels and

higher Beings in whose image he was in reality created. Tennyson
had the poetic vision to voice the true direction in which we should
be evolving:

> Let knowledge grow from more to more,
> But more of reverence in us dwell;
> That mind and soul, according well,
> May make one music as before,
>
> But vaster.[2]

"As before," that is, before mind and soul, knowledge and reverence were separated from one another by science and skepticism.
Only if we have profound reverence and feel ourselves to be a
member of the totality of the cosmos can we be conscious in the
presence of the mighty mysteries of the spirit world in the Jupiter
realm.

The Jupiter region is the mansion of our Father's house in which,
if we maintain consciousness, and if our stage of evolution warrants
it, we are able to detach ourselves from the religion we had in the
previous earthly life, and then prepare to take on a new one in the
next earthlife. Of course, some people are not able to change.
However, if it is possible to move on to a higher religious impulse,
the Jupiter realm is where one prepares for this important transformation.

The Saturn Sphere

Our cosmic journey takes us on still further to the Saturn sphere,
the realm of *cosmic memory*. In earthly life we each have our individual memory that goes back to childhood. Think of the cosmos,
too, as having a memory. Everything that ever happened in our
universe is held in memory by the Saturn Beings. That memory in its
highest form is called the Akashic Record or Chronicle, although
there is a reflection of it in the astral, or soul world, which certain
psychic persons sometimes contact. They see the reflection, but that
reflection is often distorted so that they do not get a clear picture or
true information. If one is a high enough initiate to reach into the
cosmic memory in the Saturn sphere, he sees accurately.

Everything is recorded in the Akashic Record—not only everything that our whole planetary system has experienced, but also
everything experienced by each single being in it! Because of this,
the highest righteousness of the universe, the highest cosmic-moral

forces proceed from Saturn. By preservation of the memories of the past, the spiritual-moral causal connections are maintained for human beings from earthlife to earthlife.

Consciousness in the Saturn realm depends on the degree of our *unprejudiced self-knowledge* on earth—not what opinion we had of ourselves, or what others thought of us, but what we are in reality. This implies a cosmic view of ourselves. Both the Jupiter and Saturn spheres will be experienced more consciously in the future as mankind becomes more spiritual. In these realms the spirit-germ for the head of the next life has more incorporated in it so that we can live among the Beings of the First Hierarchy, the Thrones, Cherubim, and Seraphim, just as on earth we live among animals, plants, and minerals.

It is in the Saturn sphere that we so prepare the fruit of our earthlife that it can work down into the bodily constitution in the next earthlife and manifest in childhood. If a quality is thus built into the next physical body, we say that one is a "born musician," or has an inborn understanding of spiritual science, or is a "born comedian." Such an inborn quality must have been prepared in the previous earthlife and worked over in the Saturn sphere in order to manifest in the next incarnation. It leads us to parents who provide the right heredity, e.g., a special ear structure for a musician.

In the outer planetary spheres there continues the work of metamorphosis which transforms the forces (not the substances) of the lower organism of the preceding life into the spirit-germ of the future head. By a magnificent work of metamorphosis the forces of the inner organs of one life are, as it were, turned inside out, to create the forces for the organs of the head that will be active outwardly in the next life. For example, the forces of the kidneys are transformed into the forces for the eyes; the liver bears a similar relation to the ears, as does the heart to the pineal gland, and the blood circulation to the nerves.[3]

The Zodiac

In greatest contrast to the centripetal Moon forces, the Saturn forces are the most centrifugal, and lead us out to the universe where we live with the exalted Beings of the stars. After the enormous enrichment of learning the speech of the macrocosm, and its thought and memory, we expand beyond the planetary spheres— Uranus, Neptune, and Pluto do not enter into this description for their origins differ from those of the other planets—and we enter the sphere of activity of the zodiac and even beyond the zodiac, for man as an ego-being goes beyond this "Animal Circle." "Here the work upon the primal germ of the human head, the pre-figuring and shaping of it, is brought to completion by influences pouring in from infinitudes of spiritual worlds."[4] In our age, so lacking in spiritual awareness, relatively few are conscious in this wide ocean of the cosmos where world purposes originate.

In a different description of the "spiritland," Rudolf Steiner presented an outline of the various regions in terms of the working of creative archetypes.[5] These archetypes are actual beings of the nature of thought, and they are ceaselessly active and assume myriads of forms. In the Mars sphere are the archetypes of everything physical. In the flowing life of the Jupiter realm are the archetypes of all etheric life, forming an harmonious unity. The Saturn region provides the archetypes of soul formations, or the astral world. Beyond the outer planetary spheres is a realm that orders and groups the archetypes of the Mars, Jupiter, and Saturn spheres. Here are the archetypes of human creativity, all original work of the human spirit, all manifestations of genius in any field of life. Beyond this are three more regions which might be designated as the archetypes of the archetypes, the fountainhead for the creative forces, the living germ points, the life kernels and impulses underlying all archetypes. These regions are the highest attainable by man.

The Cosmic Midnight

When we arrive at this loftiest pinnacle of macrocosmic life on our journey through the cosmos between death and rebirth, we experience what Rudolf Steiner calls the *cosmic midnight*. The midnight hour is the turning point from one day to the next. We think of it as a time of silence and of rest from daily activity. In this cosmic midnight, after all the great activity outlined earlier—working over everything personal, then universal, then cosmic—we come to a point of rest, profound inner rest. As on a mountain peak we see views in opposite directions, and as at midnight we have a meeting point of two days, now at this high elevation (figuratively speaking) not only do we look back on the preceding earthlife, or even a series of incarnations, but we also begin to look forward to a future life on the earth.

At the cosmic midnight we come to a place of decision—whether to remain in this state of bliss or to experience earthlife again and to work out our destiny. With this, there comes a longing for individual freedom which we can experience only on the earth, not in the spheres of the cosmos. This is the peak of ascent from which we begin the long descent back through the spheres in reverse order from the ascent; that is, from the zodiac, through the outer planetary spheres of Saturn, Jupiter, and Mars, on to the Sun sphere, and then through the inner planetary spheres of Venus, Mercury, and the Moon. We have seen how man becomes the cosmos; we have yet to see how the cosmos becomes man!

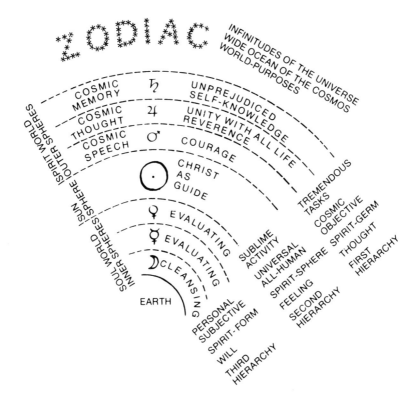

The peak of the spirit's ascent before return through the cosmos to the earth

20

THE DESCENT FROM THE ZODIAC THROUGH THE PLANETARY SPHERES IN PREPARATION FOR A NEW LIFE ON EARTH

CONSCIOUSNESS is the essential factor throughout our cosmic journey, and it depends on the consciousness we attained on earth. Our experiences in the Sun sphere are conditioned by our ego-awareness, by the universality of our feeling, and by our relation to the Christ during earthlife. We also need the connection with Christ in the outer planetary spheres where tremendous cosmic tasks await us. As we "expand" into the Mars, Jupiter, and Saturn spheres, we enter, respectively, into the realms of the cosmic word, cosmic thought, and cosmic memory, and we continue the work of metamorphosing the forces of the lower organism of the last life into the spirit-germ of the head for the next one.

In the realm of the zodiac this work of infinite grandeur proceeds, fashioning the spirit-germ for the future body in accordance with what our destiny allows, as it sounds forth from what we have inscribed in the planetary spheres. For example, after working in Aries on the future head, embodying the entire cosmos as seen from Aries, the Hierarchies in Taurus help us form the supersensible qualities of the larynx, conditioned by what shines upward and sounds forth spiritually from Mars as a result of how we used or misused our speech organs on earth. "Every untruth which a man uttered shines at him spiritually from the planet Mars while he is working through the Taurus sphere."[1]

In Gemini are elaborated the spiritual forces for the lungs, arms, hands, and symmetry; in Cancer, the rib cage, breasts, and stomach; in Leo, the heart, in harmony with what the Sun reveals of the depth and sincerity of our feelings. Virgo provides the cosmic germ for the lower metabolic organs; Libra, for the kidneys; Scorpio, the reproductive organs; Sagittarius, the hips and thighs; Capricorn, the knees; Aquarius, the calves and ankles; and Pisces, the feet. Thus, at this stage, the spirit-germ for the future body is vast and grandiose, built from the ingredients of the entire universe and the resounding influences we inscribed in the planets.

At the greatest expansion, qualitatively, in our journey between death and rebirth, there stream into our widespread being from all directions the forces of the world of the stars. While steeped in this spiritual light at the cosmic midnight, we have a clear vision of the past and the future, and a realization that our unfulfilled destiny can be corrected only on earth. With this, we have a longing to return to earth. No matter how fervently some people during earth-life assert that they do not want to return again to the earth, it is otherwise during our sojourn in the cosmos, for then we strongly wish to incarnate to correct our destiny and even to suffer to expunge our imperfections. However, on the one hand, Lucifer, who fosters pride, egotism, illusion, and a spirituality alienated from the earth, would like to entice us to remain longer in the spiritual world, or even to become a "drop-out" and not return to earth at all. On the other hand, Ahriman, who alienates one from the spirit and enslaves man to matter, tries to shorten the return journey through the cosmos, often by as much as one or two centuries. Thereby he can prevent man from "ripening" in the spiritual world, can clamp himself to the brain, take hold of thinking, and root man far too deeply in the earth.

On our outward bound journey through the cosmos, all that we experienced was determined by what we were in earthlife. On our return journey, what we receive from the cosmos depends upon our destiny. An illustration will help us to understand how something from earthlife is metamorphosed, then experienced as a new faculty in the next incarnation. Pain that we suffered on earth becomes transformed in the cosmic midnight to *will*, and that, in turn, in the next earthlife, enables us to have increased moral power. People try to avoid pain; they take tranquilizers, pain killers, anything to get rid of pain and to get over an illness quickly, not recognizing its underlying purpose. Some metaphysical movements advocate "think what you want" and promise happiness and prosperity. They do not know that the result may be a moral weakling in the next incarnation.

Having undergone the mighty metamorphosis from an earth-dweller to a vast spirit-sphere united with the cosmos and its spiritual Beings, the microcosm has "expanded" to the macrocosm. Man has become the cosmos, and now the cosmos must become man. The spirit-germ must descend through the outer planetary spheres, the Sun sphere, and the inner spheres, that is, from the realm of pure spirit, through the soul world, to the earth and into a tiny physical body. This descent demands that the wisdom of the universe be transformed into the forces for an earthly structure and that cosmic consciousness be narrowed into earthly consciousness. What a mighty metamorphosis is required from union with the cosmos and its Beings, to confinement in the small bodily organization with its shadow thoughts!

In descending through the planetary spheres, more detailed work is needed to form the wondrous cosmic spirit-germ into the cosmic pattern for the head in the next earthlife. As already noted in chapter 18, the human embryo is mostly head. The first planetary sphere on the path of return is the Saturn sphere, where on the ascent cosmic memory was experienced. Now, on the descent, the faculty of human memory is prepared. In the Jupiter sphere, instead of participating in the thoughts of the divine Beings as was done on the ascent, the spirit-germ is readied to have the faculty for conceiving human thoughts. The Mars sphere prepares us for the great gift of speech, involving work on the spiritual aspects of the speech organs, and the lungs insofar as they are connected with speech. This is an enormous and awe-inspiring task.

"If you visualize the most complicated thing that can be formed here on earth, you find it primitive and simple in contrast with the mighty fabric of cosmic vastness and grandeur which is woven there."[2] The forming of each head is "like the creation of a whole world, . . . a world of infinite variety and detail; and the work upon it calls for the devotion of human beings who are linked together by destiny, and the cooperation also of Beings of the Hierarchies who, knowing the mysteries of the cosmos, understand how such a human head must be built and formed. Wonderful it is beyond all telling, to come in this way to a knowledge of what is in man. Nor can such knowledge ever lead to pride or conceit."[3] One cannot be arrogant among the Thrones, Cherubim, and Seraphim!

Materialists on earth greatly value the physical body because they identify themselves with it and think their existence depends solely on it. As spiritual scientists, however, we value the body even more than do materialists, but for a totally different reason. We by no means identify ourselves exclusively with the body, but we know of the enormous, marvelous, cosmic activity required to create the spirit-germ for the head. Therefore we may look upon the head as "a distinct echo of our sojourn in the spiritual world."

Many years ago, my husband and I gave a series of lectures on our journey through the cosmos. A few months later we visited my parents in Ohio and went to church with them on Sunday. At the beginning of the service, the members of the choir entered the choir loft, each wearing a dark robe with a white collar; thus only the head was visible. Suddenly, the cosmic process that I had made my own in thought and feeling, I now experienced in reality. Everything else vanished as the radiant face and rounded head of one woman caught my gaze. In an almost overwhelming flash of insight, I had a most deeply moving revelation of the mighty cosmic mysteries which become incorporated in the human head. Words can give no hint of the infinitely profound impression of such an experience.

Our spirit-germ of cosmic vastness, on descending from the outer planetary spheres and entering the Sun sphere, contracts, and our consciousness is dimmed. Our activity in the outer spheres remains only as a memory, and we realize that we are no longer among the lofty Beings of the First Hierarchy. In this highly significant return passage through the Sun sphere we experience the first separation from the fullness and vastness of the cosmos as the initial foundations for the heart are laid. Interwoven with this spiritual heart is all that we are morally. We now live among the sublime Beings of the Second Hierarchy who guide the whole planetary system in relation to earth-existence. Their creative deeds stream livingly through our cosmic heart which serves as an organ of perception of the deeds of the Sun Beings. It should be noted that our physical heart during earthlife similarly is a sense organ perceiving the movement of the blood, and all that the blood contains of our conscious and unconscious experiences—a fact at variance with the modern erroneous conception of the heart as a pump. It does not pump the blood any more than the cosmic heart circulates the deeds of the Sun Beings.

The moral bundle that on our outward journey had to be "checked" in the soul world before we could rise to the spirit world, has to be picked up on the return journey through the astral world, the soul world. As a magnet attracts certain filings, so according to our moral worth, we attract astral substance out of the soul world and form a new astral body that embodies what we need for our earthly destiny.

On our return journey we choose willingly the situations that later in earthlife cause us sometimes to wonder why such things happen to us. Before birth we see the need for them, and understand how we will benefit by them; hence we accept them willingly. The time and place of birth and our ancestry are chosen long in advance, in the Sun sphere. In the Venus and Mercury spheres we align our destiny as much as possible with the outer experiences that will arise from birth into a particular nation, language, environment, family, and parents.

If people knew that we choose our parents, they would have a different attitude toward their experiences. After coming to our classes for a time, a young man came one day in a confused state and said: "You have turned my whole world upside down. I used to blame my father for my unhappy childhood. Now you say that we choose our parents." Once we accept the fact that our destiny is self-created and designed for our perfecting, we cease to blame others for our misfortunes. Sometimes we have a choice, to incarnate here or there, one life being easier and the other more difficult. From the vantage point of pre-earthly existence, we see how we will benefit more from the difficult one. We have what is called the "prenatal will." We come to birth with this prenatal will to go through the incarnation come what may! During earthlife we may forget that, but we came with it.

According to our destiny, we choose also whether we shall be male or female. To become a male we must approach the Moon sphere at the time of a New Moon, when it is light on the side of the Moon turned to the outer universe. To become a female, the descent is made at a Full Moon. If the human being who is to become a man prolongs his descent from the New to the Full Moon, he will have brown eyes and dark hair, whereas if one is to become a woman and lengthens the passage through the Moon sphere from the Full to the New Moon, she will have blue eyes and fair hair.[4] Knowledge of the normal alternation of male and female roles in successive incarnations could change considerably the attitude about women's liberation.

Not only the phases of the Moon, but also the seasons of the year are important for coming towards the earth. The four seasons are ruled successively by four archangels. Gabriel, the cosmic Archangel of the Moon, rules the season from the end of December to the beginning of spring. Only during these three months is the "door" to the earth sphere open to souls coming from the cosmos towards the earth. Even so, those who will not be born until the end of the year enter the earth sphere under Gabriel's guidance in the winter season.[5] Before conception and the forming of the etheric body, the human beings awaiting conception are enfolded only by their astral bodies. These bell-like shapes are seen, by the spiritual seer, as moving with such tremendous speed that distance is of no account.

When mankind knows how the spirit-germ is prepared in the cosmos and what occurs during the embryonic period, abortion will be seen in a different light. The precious spirit-germ, a cosmic creation, descends, is compressed, and unites with the physical germ at conception. The sense of deprivation which that causes results in gathering together in the Moon sphere a new etheric body. The suitable forces from the cosmic ether are collected by the Moon from the planets during the days of the week ruled by the respective planets.

Thou Being, offspring of worlds, who in thy light-form	(Sunday–
Art strengthened by the Sun under the Moon's control,	Monday)
Thou art endowed by Mars with his creative ringing,	(Tuesday)
Mercury bestows limbs' elastic swinging,	(Wednesday)
Jupiter illumines thee with Wisdom's glow;	(Thursday)
Love-bearing beauty Venus doth bestow—	(Friday)
And Saturn's ancient spirit-inwardness	(Saturday)
Thee consecrates to life in space, to growth in time.[6]	

Three weeks after conception, the etheric body, astral body, and ego descend, but only gradually become active: the etheric body, about the seventh week; the astral body, more intensely about the seventh month; and the ego, near birth (see page 27).

Throughout the return journey from the zodiac to incarnation, a diminution of consciousness takes place until, in the Moon sphere, it is reduced to dream consciousness. As a transformer reduces electrical current, so the Moon sphere serves as a transformer of the consciousness we still had in the Venus and Mercury spheres until it is dimmed down to the unconsciousness of dream and sleep. What do we associate with the Moon? Night, and sleep. And what does the infant do? It sleeps most of the time. It dwells in the unconsciousness of the Moon sphere in the early part of its life. The vast cosmic consciousness of the spirit-germ has to be narrowed and dimmed to enter the prison, as it were, of the physical body. Yet we bring with us all the marvelous forces we experienced in the cosmos, which Wordsworth expressed in this beautiful stanza:

> Our birth is but a sleep and a forgetting:
> The Soul that rises with us, our life's Star,
> Hath had elsewhere its setting,
> And cometh from afar:
> Not in entire forgetfulness,
> And not in utter nakedness,
> But trailing clouds of glory do we come
> From God, who is our home.[7]

Our hearts leap with joy at the awareness that as every human being, "made young again" during the long cosmic journey, arrives on the earth at birth, rejuvenating forces stream anew into our earth. What potential in the on-going process of world-becoming! If to the purely materialistic view of the human germ cells uniting and growing, we add the image of the stork, we may come closer, through picture language, to the marvelous confluence of the material stream of heredity uniting with the stream of the independent ego's journey through the cosmos with the help of divine Beings. Truly, *Ex Deo Nascimur*, out of God we are born.

The cosmic journey between death and rebirth usually takes centuries of time. The normal rhythm in past epochs was to incarnate once as a male and once as a female in each cultural age of 2,160 years, which provided new conditions on the earth. This has been speeded up considerably. We must take into consideration that there are exceptions to the general rhythm. Death at an advanced age usually results in remaining longer than average in the cosmic spheres, whereas children who die under 13 can incarnate again very quickly, sometimes into the same family. Death before 35 may also bring one back soon, with surplus capital carried over from the unused forces of the previous brief earthlife. When many die young, as in war, the loss is not as tragic as it appears outwardly, for the unused forces will be utilized when the persons, who sacrificed their lives, return relatively quickly as "a crop of geniuses." The wisdom of the cosmos thereby provides for a period of spiritual blossoming later.

There are many more aspects of the cosmic journey than have been included in these descriptions. It is hoped, however, that from what has been presented you gained new concepts that deepened your feelings. Leonardo da Vinci said, "Great love is a daughter of great knowledge." Rudolf Steiner added, "He who does not want to know does not in the true sense learn to love."[8] If we have taken these cosmic concepts into our thinking permeated with feeling, we shall have a sense of kinship with all human beings, knowing that each individual is a cosmic mystery, a confluence of the secrets of worlds and the deeds of the supersensible Beings, ranging from the Angels to the Seraphim.

Contemplation of the sublime wisdom of these Beings, and of our kinship with the whole cosmos, evokes wonder, awe, and reverence. If it then permeates the depths of our souls, it strengthens the will, for we realize that we have a responsibility to nurture what was given to us by the cosmos—a responsibility to expand it and to use it wisely for the cosmos. This has been stated in the form of a prayer: "The more conscious I become that I am born out of the Universe, and the more deeply I feel the responsibility to develop in myself the forces given to me by a whole Universe, the better human being I can become."[9] This responsibility is never a burden, for it is accompanied by ceaseless gratitude for the abundance of the cosmic bestowal, and gratitude that we can live as conscious *citizens of the cosmos.*

EPILOGUE: CONSCIENTIOUS CITIZENS
OF THE COSMOS

HUMAN NATURE will never be understood until the relation to the cosmos is recognized and comprehended. And conversely, the nature and structure of the cosmos will never be conceived rightly apart from mankind. The tendency in our century has been toward fragmentation. In order to reunite what fragmented knowledge has torn asunder, it is necessary to put into the picture of humanity and the cosmos the spiritual reality which materialistic science has not only ignored, but often denied.

Only a science of the spirit can give the complete picture of the cosmos and of man. The complete picture includes the spirituality of the cosmos, and the soul and spirit as well as the body of man. It takes into account repeated earthlives, describing both life's unfolding on earth, and the much longer sojourn in the cosmos between death and rebirth.

Knowledge of our divine origin and relation to the cosmos does not alienate us from earthlife. On the contrary, we can appreciate much more the new opportunities each earthlife presents, and we learn to value the rhythmic alternation between life on earth and in the superearthly realms of the cosmos. Such knowledge is mankind's urgent need today. It is the lifesaving alternative to submersion in materialism and subjection to mechanization. It is a guarantee against accepting, or being victimized by, the menacing trends that would rob us of our cosmic and human heritage, and would manipulate and mold us from outside as if we had no soul and spirit inside.

The urgent need of this Michael Age is to *spiritualize the intelligence,* which the dragon has made shrewd and cold. Far from shunning earthlife, we work arduously to aid Michael, the Archangel of the Sun, who points to the Christ and is the proclaimer of the cosmic Christ. We cooperate with Michael and the Christ in creating the world anew.

> Imbue us with your mighty solar power
> To turn the tide this serious, fateful hour!
> May we, awake, full-armed in freedom's light

> Defend the Earth against the dragon's blight.
> The Ahrimanic intellect is shrewd,
> Our spirit weapons should be sharp, not crude;
> The enemy is subtle, sly, and cold,
> Inhuman, yet in humans he takes hold
> And tries to make them into a machine
> And thus promote his standardizing scheme
> To mold all in a pattern uniform
> Of earthly style, away from Cosmos torn.
> The Living Essence of the Christ be ours
> To match against these Ahrimanic powers!
> The life-blood of the universe and man
> Flow livingly through us, so that we can
> Become true Michaelites, with iron will,
> The mission of our Age to help fulfill.

Knowledge of our spiritual nature and our relation to the spirituality of the cosmos is especially needed to reeducate mankind to an awareness that we live in a universe in which moral laws are as real as natural laws. When the spirituality of the cosmos is lost, morality is lost. Morality is not something imposed from outside. It arises from an enlightened recognition and activity of soul and spirit. Morality will be inherent if we live as conscious citizens of the cosmos.

In various ways—in psychology, psychiatry, encounter groups, how-to courses—sincere efforts are being made to attain self-knowledge. Life's unfolding and our cosmic journey reveal that complete self-knowledge is attained only through world-knowledge. This is epitomized in these lines:

> If you would know your Self,
> Look out into the Cosmic Spaces.
> If you would fathom the Cosmic Spaces,
> Look inwards, into your own Self.[1]

With this cosmic comprehension, we lose all apprehension. For we know and feel, with a conviction and confidence that carry us through every crisis, that we are citizens of the cosmos.

Courageously, in freedom, we tread the earth; we walk in the light, and radiate light. With serenity, and with alert readiness for insightful, love-filled, innovative activity, we participate—each in one's own unique way—in the continuing creativity of the cosmos, as conscious, conscientious *citizens of the cosmos.*[2]

NOTES

Chapter 2: Changing Consciousness and Changing World-Pictures

Rudolf Steiner, *Christ and the Spiritual World*, Leipzig, 1913–14; Rudolf Steiner Press, London.
——, *Karmic Relationships*, Vol. III, Dornach, Switzerland, 1924; Vol. VIII, England, 1924 (formerly *Cosmic Christianity*); Anthroposophical Publishing Co., London.
——, *The Mission of the Archangel Michael*, 1918–19; Anthroposophic Press, New York.
John Meeks, *Cosmic Rhythms and the Course of History*, in *The Golden Blade* 1979; Rudolf Steiner Press, London.

Chapter 3: Planetary Laws

1. Steiner, *True and False Paths in Spiritual Investigation*, Lecture 6, Torquay, England, August 1924; Rudolf Steiner Press, London.
2. ——, *The Problems of Our Time*, Lecture 2, Berlin, September 1919; Anthroposophic Press, New York.

Chapter 4: Earthlife Begins

1. Frederick LeBoyer, *Birth Without Violence*, 1978; Alfred A. Knopf, New York.
2. Steiner, *The Spiritual Guidance of Man*, Lecture 3, Copenhagen, June 1911; Anthroposophic Press, New York.
3. ——, *The Concealed Aspects of Human Existence*, The Hague, November 3, 1922; New York.
4. R. Lissau, "Comment" in *Anthroposophical Quarterly*, Winter 1972; Rudolf Steiner Press, London.
5. Steiner, *Man: Hieroglyph of the Universe*, Lecture 3, April 1920; Anthroposophic Press, New York.
6. Norbert Glas, M.D., *Conception, Birth and Early Childhood*, Anthroposophic Press, New York.
7. Steiner, *The Education of the Child*, Rudolf Steiner Press, London.
8. Eva A. Frommer, *Voyage Through Childhood into the Adult World*, Pergamon Press.

9. Steiner, *The Spiritual Guidance of Man*, Copenhagen, 1911; Anthroposophic Press, New York.
10. Karl König, *The First Three Years of the Child*, Anthroposophic Press, New York.
11. Ibid.
12. Steiner, *Education of the Child*.
13. Steiner, *Lectures to Teachers*, 1921.
14. A. C. Harwood, *The Recovery of Man in Childhood*, Hodder and Stoughton, London.
15. Steiner, *Lectures to Teachers*.
16. ———, *The Kingdom of Childhood*, Torquay, England, August 1924; Rudolf Steiner Press, London.
17. ———, *The Roots of Education*, Berne, April 1924; Rudolf Steiner Press, London.
18. ———, *Lectures to Teachers*.
19. ———, *Education of the Child*.
20. ———, *Lectures to Teachers*.

Chapter 5: The Mercury Cycle

1. Steiner, *Earth and Stars*, September 20, 1924; not published in English.
2. ———, *The Kingdom of Childhood*, page 57.

Valuable Source Material
Steiner, *The Study of Man*, Anthroposophic Press, New York.
Child and Man, Winter 1972, July 1973, January 1974, July 1974.
Marjorie Spock, *Teaching as a Lively Art*, Anthroposophic Press, New York.
Lois Cusick, *Waldorf Parenting Handbook*, Gainesville, Florida.
References listed in the previous chapter should also be consulted.

Chapter 6: The Venus Cycle

1. L. Francis Edmunds, *Rudolf Steiner Education*, a "Child and Man" Publication.
2. *Curriculum of the First Waldorf School*, Steiner Schools Fellowship, England.

Valuable Source Material
Child and Man, July 1973 and January 1974.
Steiner, *Education as a Social Problem*, Dornach, August 1919; Anthroposophic Press, New York.
———, *The Modern Art of Education*, Ilkley, England, August 1923; Rudolf Steiner Press, London.
———, *Spiritual Ground of Education*, Oxford, England, August 1922; Anthroposophical Publishing Company, London (later, Rudolf Steiner Press).
———, *Human Values in Education*, Arnheim, July 1924; Anthroposophic Press, New York.

Chapter 7: Three Seven-Year Sun Cycles

1. Steiner, "The Mission of Anger" in *Metamorphoses of the Soul*, Berlin, October 21, 1909; Anthroposophic Press, New York.
2. ———, *Theosophy: An Introduction to Supersensible Knowledge*, chapter 1, part 2, Anthroposophic Press, New York.
3. Grant Lewi, *Astrology for the Millions*, Llewellyn Publications, St. Paul, Minnesota.
4. Steiner, *The Course of My Life*, Chapter 10 (new title, *Rudolf Steiner, An Autobiography*), Rudolf Steiner Publications, New York.
5. Ibid.
6. Ibid., chapter 11.
7. Steiner, *The Fifth Gospel*, Rudolf Steiner Press, London.
8. Ormond Edwards, *A New Chronology of the Gospels*, Floris Books, Edinburgh.
9. Ibid.
10. Steiner, *Background to the Gospel of St. Mark*, Lecture 4, Berlin, December 6, 1910; Rudolf Steiner Press, London, page 65.
11. ———, *Theosophy, An Introduction to Supersensible Knowledge*, Chapter 1, part 4.
12. Steiner, *The Apocalypse of St. John*, Lecture 12, Nuremberg, June 1908; Rudolf Steiner Press, London.
13. ———, *Macrocosm and Microcosm*, Lecture 11, Vienna, March 1910; Rudolf Steiner Press, London.
14. Mary Fullerson, *By a New and Living Way*, Stuart & Watkins, London, page 68.
15. Steiner, *Guidance in Esoteric Training*, Rudolf Steiner Press, London.
16. ———, *The Course of My Life*, Chapters 26 and 27.
17. Ibid.
18. Steiner, *The Philosophy of Spiritual Activity*, chapter 12; Rudolf Steiner Publications, New York.
19. Tennyson, *In Memoriam*, CXIV.
20. Steiner, *Calendar of the Soul*, stanza 41; Rudolf Steiner Press, London.
21. ———, *The Mysteries of the East and of Christianity*, Lecture 4, Berlin 1913; Rudolf Steiner Press, London.
22. Tennyson, "Gareth and Lynette," *Idylls of the King*.
23. Goethe, *Faust*, part I, l. 1112.

Chapter 8: The Mars Cycle

1. Steiner, *The Problems of Our Time*, chapter 2; Berlin, September 1919, Anthroposophic Press, New York.
2. ———, *Theosophy: An Introduction to Supersensible Knowledge*, chapter I, part 4; Anthroposophic Press, New York.
3. Robert Browning, "Rabbi Ben Ezra", 1.3.
4. Steiner, *Karmic Relationships*, Vol. II, chapter 11; Rudolf Steiner Press, London.
5. ———, *The Remedy for Our Diseased Civilization*, August 6, 1921; not published in English.
6. ———, *The Festivals and Their Meaning*, Vol. IV, Michaelmas, "The

Significance of the Impulse of Michael", October 15, 1923; Rudolf Steiner Press, London.

7. Ibid.
8. Wilhelm Pelikan, *The Secrets of Metals*, chapter 5 on Iron, Anthroposophic Press, New York.
9. Tennyson, *In Memoriam* CXVIII.
10. ———, *Sir Galahad*.
11. Guenther Wachsmuth, *The Life and Work of Rudolf Steiner*, Whittier Books, Inc., New York.
12. Ibid.

Chapter 9: The Jupiter Cycle

1. Steiner, *The Spiritual Individualities of the Planets*, July 27, 1923, published in *The Golden Blade* 1966; Rudolf Steiner Press, London.
2. Wordsworth, "ODE: Intimations of Immortality from Recollections of Early Childhood," ll. 179–187.
3. Romans 8:28.
4. Psalm 8:5.
5. Steiner, *The Christ Impulse and the Development of Ego Consciousness*, Berlin 1909; Anthroposophic Press, New York.
6. ———, *Theosophy: An Introduction to Supersensible Knowledge*, chapter 1, part 4.
7. Wachsmuth, *The Life and Work of Rudolf Steiner*.
8. John C. Agers, *A Short Biography of Emanuel Swedenborg*, Swedenborg Foundation, New York.

Chapter 10: The Saturn Cycle

1. Steiner, *Occult Science—An Outline*, chapter 7, 1910; Anthroposophic Press, New York.
2. ———, *Karmic Relationships*, Vol. II, Lecture 11, 1924.
3. Pelikan, *The Secrets of Metals*, chapter 3 on Lead.
4. Ibid.
5. Wachsmuth, *The Life and Work of Rudolf Steiner*.

Chapter 11: The Uranus Cycle

1. Steiner, *True and False Paths in Spiritual Investigation*, end of chapter 6, August 1924, London.
2. Adam Bittleston, *The Golden Blade*, 1976, London, page 47.
3. Wachsmuth, *The Life and Work of Rudolf Steiner*.

Chapter 12: The Neptune Cycle

1. Steiner, *Man: Hieroglyph of the Universe*, Lecture 4, 1920; Rudolf Steiner Press, London; also *Cosmic and Human Metamorphoses*, Lecture 2, Berlin, 1917; Anthroposophical Publishing Company, London.

2. ———, *Karmic Relationships*, Vol. III, Lecture 3, 1924; London.
3. ———, *Man's Life on Earth and in the Spiritual World*, Last Lecture, England, 1922; London.
4. ———, *Metamorphoses of the Soul*, Lecture 3, Berlin, 1909; Anthroposophic Press, New York.
5. ———, *Earthly and Cosmic Man*, Lecture 6, Berlin, 1912; Rudolf Steiner Publishing Company, London.
6. Norbert Glas, *The Fulfillment of Old Age*, New York.

Chapter 13: The Pluto Cycle

1. V. Elenbaas, *Focus on Pluto*.
2. W. Sucher, *Practical Approach Towards a New Astrosophy;* Meadow Vista, California, page 41.
3. Robert Browning, "Rabbi Ben Ezra".
4. Faith Baldwin, "My Crabbéd Age," *Reader's Digest*, July 1977.
5. Martha Childers Humbard, *Give Me That Old-Time Religion;* Logos International, page 16.
6. Steiner, *Earthly and Cosmic Man*, Lecture 6, Berlin, 1912; Rudolf Steiner Publishing Company, London.
7. ———, *Conscience and Astonishment*, in *The Golden Blade* 1967, Rudolf Steiner Press, London.
8. ———, *From Jesus to Christ*, Lecture 10, Carlsruhe, 1911; Rudolf Steiner Press, London.

Chapter 14: The Portal of Death

1. Elizabeth Kübler-Ross, *On Death and Dying*, Macmillan, New York.
2. Raymond A. Moody, Jr., *Life After Life*, Mockingbird Books, 1976.
3. ———, *Life After Life, and Reflections on Life After Life*, Guideposts, Carmel, New York.
4. Steiner, *From Jesus to Christ*, Lecture 10, Carlsruhe, 1911; Rudolf Steiner Press, London.
5. ———, *Verses and Meditations*, London, page 199.
6. Tennyson, "Gareth and Lynette," *Idylls of the King*.
7. Steiner, Last lines of *A Meditation for the Departed*.
8. ———, *On the Meaning of Life*, Lecture 1, Copenhagen, 1912; Anthroposophical Publishing Company, London.
9. Wachsmuth, *The Life and Work of Rudolf Steiner*.
10. Steiner, *The Problems of Our Time*, Chapter 2, Berlin, September 1919; Anthroposophic Press, New York.

Part II

The chapters are the outgrowth of lectures begun in the 1950s, and were published, as a series of articles, between Easter 1972 and June 1973. They were then revised in 1980, and combined with the very first series circulated in 1951.

Chapter 15: Overcoming Barriers to Spiritual Understanding

Valuable Source Material

BOOKS BY RUDOLF STEINER

Supersensible Man, given at The Hague, November 1923; Anthroposophical Publishing Co., London

The Human Being, His Destiny, and World Evolution, Oslo, May 1923; Anthroposophic Press, New York

Theosophy: An Introduction to Supersensible Knowledge, 1904; Anthroposophic Press, New York

Occult Science—An Outline, 1910; Anthroposophic Press, New York

Life Between Death and Rebirth, October 1912–May 1913; Anthroposophic Press, New York

Man's Life on Earth and in the Spiritual Worlds, given in England 1922; Anthroposophical Publishing Co., London

Between Death and Rebirth, November 1912–April 1913; Rudolf Steiner Press, London

The Inner Nature of Man and Life Between Death and Rebirth, Vienna, April 1914; Anthroposophical Publishing Co., London

The Forming of Destiny and Life After Death, Berlin, November–December 1915; Anthroposophical Publishing Co., London

The Theosophy of the Rosicrucians, Munich, May–June 1907; Rudolf Steiner Publishing Co., London

Rosicrucian Esotericism, Budapest, June 1909; Anthroposophic Press, New York

Karmic Relationships, Vol. V., Prague and Paris, March–May, 1924; Rudolf Steiner Press, London

PAMPHLETS BY RUDOLF STEINER

Links between the Living and the Dead, Bergen, October 1913; London

The Dead Are With Us, Nuremberg, February 1918; London

The Concealed Aspects of Human Existence and the Christ Impulse, The Hague, November 1922; New York

Occult Research into Life between Death and a New Birth, Stuttgart, February 1913; New York

BOOKS BY OTHER AUTHORS

Stanley Drake, *Though You Die,* Floris Books, Edinburgh

Guenther Wachsmuth, *Reincarnation as a Phenomenon of Metamorphosis,* Anthroposophic Press, New York

Raymond A. Moody, Jr., M.D., *Life After Life, and Reflections on Life After Life,* Guideposts, Carmel, N.Y.

Chapter 16: At the Departure Gate

1. Steiner, *From Jesus to Christ,* Lecture 3 and 10.
2. Moody, *Life After Life, and Reflections on Life After Life.*

Chapter 18: The Sun Sphere

1. Steiner, *Supersensible Man*, Lecture 3.

Chapter 19: The Outer Planetary Spheres

1. Steiner, *Life between Death and Rebirth*, Lecture 11, March 2, 1912; Anthroposophic Press, New York; *Man in the Light of Occultism, Theosophy, and Philosophy*, Lectures 9 and 10, given in Norway, June 1912; Rudolf Steiner Press, London.
2. Tennyson, *In Memoriam* (Introduction).
3. Steiner, *Man: Hieroglyph of the Universe*, Dornach, Switzerland, 1920; Rudolf Steiner Press, London.
4. ———, *Supersensible Man*, The Hague, November 1923; London.
5. ———, *Theosophy: An Introduction to Supersensible Knowledge*, 1904; New York.

Chapter 20: Descent from the Zodiac

1. Steiner, *Man's Life on Earth and in the Spiritual Worlds*, Lecture 6, England, 1922; London.
2. ———, *The Concealed Aspects of Human Existence*, The Hague, November 1922; New York.
3. ———, *Supersensible Man*, Lecture 4, The Hague, November 1923; London.
4. ———, *Concealed Aspects*.
5. ———, *The Four Seasons and the Archangels*, Lecture 5, Dornach, Switzerland, October 13, 1923; London.
6. ———, *The Festival of Easter*, Lecture 4, Dornach, April 22, 1924; Rudolf Steiner Press, London.
7. Wordsworth, "Ode: Intimations of Immortality," ll. 58–65.
8. Steiner, *Between Death and Rebirth*, Lecture 9, Berlin, March 4, 1913; London, page 168.
9. ———, *Life between Death and Rebirth*, Lecture 3, Hanover, November 18, 1912; New York, page 53.

Epilogue

1. Steiner, *Karmic Relationships*, Vol. VII, Lecture 2, Breslau, June 8, 1924; London, page 35.
2. Beredene Jocelyn, *At the Departure Gate with a Citizen of the Cosmos*, A Supplement to *Citizens of the Cosmos*, St. George Publications, Spring Valley, New York, 1981.

Beredene Jocelyn was a leader of several anthroposophic study groups in the New York City area, and worked throughout her life to bring Anthroposophy into the world. She wrote several books, including *At the Departure Gate with a Citizen of the Cosmos,* and edited a monthly newsletter. She was married to John Jocelyn, author of *Meditations on the Signs of the Zodiac.*

Breinigsville, PA USA
10 March 2010
233902BV00001B/10/P